PLAYS WITHOUT ENDINGS

Tough Choices

GLOBE FEARON EDUCATIONAL PUBLISHER
A Division of Simon & Schuster
Upper Saddle River, New Jersey

Project Editor: Lynn W. Kloss
Editorial Assistant: Kristen Shepos
Editorial Supervisor: Steven Otfinoski
Production Manager: Penny Gibson
Production Editor: Linda Greenberg
Marketing Manager: Sandra Hutchison
Interior Electronic Design and Art Supervision: Joan Jacobus
Electronic Page Production: José A. López
Illustrator: Allen Davis
Cover Design: Patricia Smythe
Cover Illustration: © Jerry McDaniel '94

Printed in the United States of America.
4 5 6 7 8 9 10 99 98

ISBN: 0-835-91198-5

GLOBE FEARON EDUCATIONAL PUBLISHER
A Division of Simon & Schuster
Upper Saddle River, New Jersey

Contents

About This Book

This book can be an adventure. Within its pages are people who must decide whether to join gangs, betray a friend, take a chance on love, or even risk their lives.

The best part, though, is the ending that you write. In most plays, the author decides what happens. In these plays, you decide whether the characters will do the right thing or take the easy way out. It's in your hands.

As you read these plays, think about how you might handle the situations. Think about what others you know might do if faced with that problem. You might consider a completely new solution. Use your imagination to think up the perfect, unexpected ending.

As you think about the ending you'll write, though, remember that you're writing for characters in a play, not for yourself. Try to make the decision you think the character might make.

Some of these characters may face unpleasant situations you recognize. If the plot of one play makes you uncomfortable, you might want to finish another one instead. It is possible, though, that thinking about the situation the character faces may provide you with some new ways of dealing with problems in your life.

You can also find ways to finish these plays by talking over the situation with friends, parents, or brothers and sisters. Play the scene out in your mind and "see" what might happen next. You could try different endings to see which one works best. You might also get together with a friend and read the play aloud, trying out different endings.

Above all, have fun. Relax and let your imagination take over. You might even surprise yourself.

Serena

by Chiori Santiago

Characters:
Serena
Tanya

Scene: *a high school courtyard in front of a building with a flight of steps leading to the entrance. Serena enters, carrying books. She walks slowly, looking once over her shoulder. A moment later, Tanya appears and walks down the steps toward Serena.*

TANYA: Hey, Serena, what's the matter? Why did you walk out like that?

SERENA: I have, um . . . an appointment, that's all. I have to leave a little early.

TANYA: What appointment are you talking about? I know you didn't make any appointment for the same day as the nominations meeting. Girl, you've been wanting to be an official member of the African American Students League since school started. And now you're nominated, girl! *[She sits down next to Serena.]* What's up?

SERENA: No, it's nothing. It's just that . . . you know how sometimes you want something really bad, and then by the time you get it, it doesn't seem so special after all? Like maybe you outgrow it. Like when we were little, we all wanted Topper dolls, and everyone had one except me. I couldn't get one until Christmas. When I got one, I was so happy. But then about a month later,

1

the doll's eyelashes fell out, and the clothes got kind of torn up, and it didn't seem so great anymore.

TANYA: Oh, please, Serena, we're not talking about kiddie toys; we're talking about the most important club in the whole school. I mean, the African American Students League! It's where things get done. It's the cream of the crop. You don't get in without a B average, and all the best people get pledged. *[She ticks off names on her fingers.]* Sammy Phelps, captain of the football team; Liddy Browning, only the best speechmaker this school has ever seen; Misha Jackson, school newspaper; LaVon White, student rep for the rally in Washington; and that's just the seniors. I mean, the league is a real force around here. We teach kids about the political process, we get out the vote, we volunteer, we make the school proud. Last year, Congressman Watson came to us for an endorsement! That's the kind of pull we have——not to mention some of the finest-looking men in the school. What's your problem?

SERENA: Tanya, you've known me forever. Don't make me have to explain.

TANYA: You'd better start explaining.

SERENA: Well, it's the boycott. The one Morris was talking about.

TANYA: Oh, that old thing? The one about boycotting corner stores? It'll be a long time before that even gets organized. Don't worry about it.

SERENA: Not any stores. Asian-owned stores.

TANYA: Oh. Yeah. *[Both are silent.]* It's not like he doesn't have a point. Anyway, you just have to understand where Morris is coming from. A lot of black folks just don't like those Asian groceries.

SERENA: They've been there for years.

TANYA: That's the problem. They open up in our neighborhoods, making a lot of money selling us beer and cigarettes so we can get lung cancer and drink ourselves to death. At the end of the day they close up, get in their Mercedes, and drive home to the suburbs. You don't see them spending money in *our* businesses. In fact, if they didn't drain our neighborhoods of the money we earn, you might see more African Americans owning businesses.

SERENA: I can't believe I'm hearing you say this. That's pretty racist.

TANYA: Serena, I'm just stating a fact.

SERENA: Think about this fact: What about my mother?

TANYA: Serena, those kids don't know your mother's Japanese. You look just like one of us. Besides, your mother doesn't own a corner store.

SERENA: That's not the point, and you know it. Listen, of

course I want to be part of the league. It's what I've been working for this whole year. That's why I did all the volunteer work. But I did it because I believed in it, too. I live in this neighborhood. Don't you think I see what goes on? We need to get out and vote. We need to help the kids. We need people to help with the second-grade reading program and after-school basketball. I just don't see why my people need to team up against some other people. We should be promoting unity, not dividing people.

TANYA: Listen to what you just said: "My people." You're black, Serena, just like me and everyone else in the league. That's who we're helping, our people.

SERENA: But my people are Asian, too.

TANYA: But the boycott isn't saying all Asians are bad. We're just protesting against the store owners who come in, don't even speak our language, and don't hire us. If you go asking them for a job, right there in your own community, they always say [*mimicking*]: "So sorry! My uncle, my nephew, my son need a job." Those folks have more relatives than your little brother has guppies.

SERENA: OK, so there are some problems. But that's just how Asian families operate. And I don't see any African Americans hurrying to hire Asians—or whites, for that matter. People stick to themselves.

TANYA: That's human nature.

SERENA: Yeah? So where does that leave me?

TANYA: All right, so there are a few people who break the mold. Your mom's been like a mother to me. Remember how we used to go to your house every day after school, and she always fixed fried rice? I thought that was so cool. It was like having a take-out restaurant in your own home. I've never thought of your mother as different—I really forget your mother is Japanese. Except when she used to call me Tan-chan. Boy, that little nickname cracked me up. Anyway, she's been married to your father so long and living in this neighborhood so long, she's like one of us.

SERENA: But she is Japanese. And for me to join the league and be part of this boycott—don't you see I just couldn't do it? I couldn't turn against part of myself.

TANYA: Someday, you'll have to choose. Listen, my great-granddaddy was white. Does that make me white? No. Anyone who looks at me is going to think: African American. That's who I am, that's who my parents are, and that's who you are, too. Anyone who looks at you—and I'm talking about all the kids in the league—will see you as a sister. A fine black sister. You should be proud of that.

SERENA: Of course I'm proud. But I'm proud of both my parents. I wish I could explain it, Tanya. Maybe I think of myself more as African American because I grew up in this neighborhood. When I was little, I didn't want other kids to know my mother ate yellow pickles with rice. I didn't want them to laugh at me. I wanted to be like everyone else. And you're right: When folks look at me they never think I'm half Japanese—never. I just fit right in, and it's fine. I like that. But that doesn't mean I'm not proud of being half Japanese. *[She thinks a minute.]* What if I just admitted how I feel? I can't be part of the boycott. But what if I got up and said we could meet with some of the store owners?

TANYA: You, Serena? That sure doesn't sound like you. You mean you're going to make life harder on yourself by admitting, number one, that you're half Japanese and, number two, telling the activities committee to change their minds completely?

SERENA: Sure. The league could tell the store owners how

we feel about jobs. Or maybe we could ask them to donate to something, like the after-school reading program. They could help buy books. Why can't Asians and African Americans just get together on something? It could happen.

TANYA: I don't know, Serena. It's never happened before, not that I know of. *[She puts an arm around her friend.]* Why don't you think about the risks? You could miss out on a chance to be part of the league, and that means a lot. Besides, we can't change the whole world.

SERENA: Isn't that what the league is all about?

TANYA: Look, Serena. If I were you, I wouldn't make such a big deal out of this boycott. You're one of us. We're always going to accept you. Do those Asian store owners look at you as one of theirs? I never saw one of them walk up to you and say, "Sister!" Come on. Be part of us. Don't make an easy decision hard.

SERENA: *[She sits and thinks for a moment and then gives her friend a quick hug.]* Let's go back inside, Tanya. I know what I'm going to do. I'll . . .

IIIII THINKING ABOUT THE PLAY

1. Why does Serena walk out of the meeting at the beginning of the play?

2. Why hasn't Serena revealed that she is half Japanese to the group?

3. Do you think Tanya is supportive of Serena? Give examples to back up your answer.

4. Do you think people with a mixed heritage should choose to be part of one group? Why or why not?

5. Because Serena understands the complaints students have against the store owners, should she support the boycott? Explain.

Serena must decide whether to join the league and support a boycott she doesn't agree with or question the boycott and risk her membership in the league. In making her decision, she may have to reveal something about her racial identity that she feels is private, and she may have to stand up against a group she wants very much to belong to.

Using what you know about Serena, write an ending that shows whether she stands up against the boycott or supports it and joins the league. You might also have Serena choose some other course of action. Include in your ending what happens to Serena as a result of her decision.

Alexandra

by Cecilia Rubino

Characters:
Alexandra
Liz
Alexandra's Mother

Scene: *late in the evening. Liz is finishing her homework when she hears someone knocking at the front door.*

ALEX: *[whispering]* Liz! Liz, it's me, Alex. Let me in.

LIZ: Alex? *[Liz opens the door and gives her friend a hug.]* Alex, are you all right? Everybody is looking for you.

ALEX: *[nervously]* I didn't want to ring the buzzer. Is your mother home?

LIZ: She's at the hospital. She doesn't get off work till late. Don't worry: my dad and Ralph are already asleep. Where were you? It's been almost a week. Why didn't you call me? We've been so worried.

ALEX: I couldn't talk. *[rubbing her bruised forehead]* I didn't want anyone to see me like this.

LIZ: Alex, I'm so sorry. Jack really beat you, didn't he?

ALEX: He found out I was seeing Ray. The man is not even my father, and nobody I hang out with is good enough for him. They're too old, they're going to get me in trouble, they're no good. I mean, Jack has something to say about *everyone.* Are you sure nobody else is here?

LIZ: Nobody's here. Alex, are you OK? Your mother's going crazy trying to find you.

ALEX: Good; serves her right. It would serve her right if they found me dead somewhere, and then she would have to live with that the rest of her life.

LIZ: Come on; don't say that.

ALEX: It's true. You heard the fight?

LIZ: Everybody on the block heard the fight. People said Ray broke your stepfather's arm.

ALEX: After he saw what Jack did to me, Ray went after him with a baseball bat. The cops came. They were going to take Ray in. Jack had to go to the hospital. They wanted to take me to the hospital, too, for the cut on my head, but I said no. I couldn't stand being anywhere near that man. And all the time my mother is screaming about me, saying, "It's her fault, she started this, going out with that scum."

LIZ: I can't believe this happened.

ALEX: You know, Ray and I had been keeping it kind of quiet. Then a couple of nights ago I'm on the phone, and Jack comes in. When he finds out it's Ray, he pulls the phone out of the wall.

LIZ: Out of the wall?

ALEX: That's the way Jack is. Sometimes he just goes off. And then he really started to give it to me. I had to run out of the house. I mean I ran out in my nightgown and walked all the way to Ray's in my bare feet. The next day, I called my mother and I said, "I can't stay in that man's house anymore. I'm afraid of what he's going to do to me." I said, "Ma, I've got to come and get some of my things for a while. I need my books for school and my clothes." I had to borrow clothes from Ray. But I told her I couldn't come when Jack was there.

LIZ: You're mother's been so upset. She's been here crying. I feel so bad for her.

ALEX: *[bitterly]* You listen to what she did. I called her that night, and she told me he was out of the house. But the whole thing was a set-up. She lied, she out-and-out lied to me. I walked in the door, and he was waiting right there to grab me. She helped him get me into my room. She stood there and let him hit me like that. She didn't do anything.

LIZ: I'm so sorry. I can't believe he hurt you like that.

ALEX: That man has been going after me since the day he moved in with us. He hits me, he hits her, and she doesn't do anything to stop it. Remember when she went to the hospital around Christmastime?

LIZ: She sprained her arm?

ALEX: *Jack* sprained her arm. They had a fight about me. Every time something happens, my mother always says things are going to change, but nothing ever does. It just happens again. And she says, "Oh, you just never liked him, and that's why he gets mad," and "He's so good to you; he just wants you to behave."

LIZ: You never told me he hit you.

ALEX: When I was younger, he'd hit me for anything. I always thought it was my fault. I guess I thought it was normal. I'd talk back or I'd spill something; maybe he'd be drunk and wham!

LIZ: Why didn't you ever say anything?

ALEX: I didn't know how to tell anybody. I remember one time in gym I couldn't even sit cross-legged because he hit me so bad. The teacher asked me what was wrong, but I didn't know what to say. I mean, I guess I thought it was my fault. Your father never hits you? He's so strict.

LIZ: He's never hit us. He threw a shoe at me once. One time, he was so mad at Ralph for running into the street, he said he was going to get his belt if it happened again. I remember going in later, Ralph and I, and opening up his drawer to look at this brand-new red leather belt and imagining what it would be like to get hit with that—but he never took it out.

ALEX: I thought it was me. I guess I thought I deserved it. I was being bad. I got into trouble a lot. I didn't want other people to know how bad I was. I still feel like it's my fault.

LIZ: It's not your fault, Alexandra. It's not.

ALEX: Things were better for a long time. Jack was going to AA meetings, my mother was going to some other kind of meeting, I was doing OK. But then everything fell apart all at the same time. Jack had that accident at work, you know, when the guy ran into him with the forklift, and he had to get his leg stitched up.

LIZ: I thought he got laid off.

ALEX: He did. Right when he was out with his leg, the airline started laying guys off, and he couldn't get his old job back. So he's just been sitting around. Now Mom is working all the time. Then they found out I was seeing Ray.

LIZ: But where'd you go after it happened? I mean, I went looking for you and you weren't even at Ray's house.

ALEX: When the cops took Ray in, I thought they weren't going to let him out. I didn't have anywhere to go. So I spent the night and all the next day just riding the trains. I didn't know where to go. I couldn't stop crying. I'd be sitting there on the train, I couldn't stop thinking about everything, and in front of all those people I'd just start to cry again. After that, I went to Ray's, but he was supposed to keep it quiet. I didn't want my mother to find me.

LIZ: Tell me what I can do, Alexandra. I feel so bad for you.

ALEX: *[crying again]* I don't know, Lizzie, I don't know. I can't sleep. When I do, all I dream about is him coming at me. I can't eat, I'm crying all the time. I can stay for a while with Ray, but I'm not ready to live there. I've got to get it together. I need my stuff for school.

LIZ: Alexandra, you know you can come and stay here. My parents would be totally fine about that.

ALEX: I can't. I'm too scared. Every time I set foot on this block, I think I'm going to see him and it'll happen all over again. Ray says I should press charges, but I don't want another scene. I just want to disappear. I don't want to fight anymore.

[The buzzer rings, startling both girls.]

ALEX: I've got to get out of here. Don't open it, Lizzie.

LIZ: Don't worry, let me just go see who it is.

ALEX 's MOTHER: Liz, Liz! Are you there? Mrs. Menna said she saw Alexandra on the block a few minutes ago. She said she came in here. *[crying]* Please Liz, please help me, I'm her mother. I just want to see Alexandra. I just want to talk to her. Everything's going to change. I don't care about Ray. I promise. I just want her back. *[knocking frantically]* Please let me in, Liz! I have to talk to you! She's my only daughter. Just tell me if you've seen her!

LIZ: . . .

1. Why doesn't Alexandra tell anyone about her stepfather's behavior?
2. Why do you think Jack behaves the way he does?
3. Why do you think Alexandra's mother allows her husband to hit her daughter?
4. Why does Alex say that everything at home fell apart at the same time?
5. Where else could Alex have gone for help?

IIII THINKING ABOUT THE ENDING

Liz has just learned some very disturbing things about Alexandra's family. Does she decide to let Alexandra's mother in, or does she lie to her about where her daughter is?

Write an ending for the play in which you include Liz's response to Alexandra's mother and how the other characters react to it. Use what you've learned about the characters to craft the ending.

Who's Got the Keys?

by Steven Otfinoski

Characters:
Tommy
Kim
Jamal
Lisa
Hank

Scene: a suburban street at night. Tommy and his friends Hank, Lisa, Jamal, and Kim have just left a party at a friend's house. They are walking to Tommy's car.

HANK: That was one crazy time, huh, Tom?

TOMMY: *[throwing an arm around Hank's shoulder]* It was the best party since your parents went away for the weekend, buddy!

KIM: Dave really knows how to throw a party.

JAMAL: Yeah. Lots of beer and good music.

LISA: Don't remind me of the beer, please. I drank *way* too much.

[Tommy awkwardly fishes out his car keys from his pocket. He starts to open the door on the driver's side.]

LISA: Let's get going. My parents will *kill* me if I'm not back by midnight.

TOMMY: *[fiddling with the lock]* Wrong key—again!
[As Tommy fumbles with the keys, he drops them into the street.] Great! Now where did they go?

[Tommy gets down on his hands and knees to find the keys. Jamal and Kim exchange glances.]

JAMAL: Tommy, are you OK?

TOMMY: Yeah, I'm OK. I just dropped the stupid keys. Help me look for them.

KIM: He means are you OK to drive?

TOMMY: Of course I am!

LISA: You had a lot of beer, Tom. Maybe you shouldn't drive.

[Tommy gets up from the ground and gives Lisa a hard look.]

TOMMY: You think I'm drunk?

JAMAL: Not drunk. Maybe a little buzzed, that's all. How do you feel?

TOMMY: I feel fine! I could drink anyone here under the table. Tell them, Hank.

HANK: You can handle your booze, all right. I remember that time out at the lake. You drank a six-pack and then drove back through the woods in the dark like a race-car driver. I still don't know how you did it.

TOMMY: See? You guys can relax. Now where are the keys?

[Kim bends over and picks up the keys at her feet.]

KIM: Here they are.

TOMMY: Great. Give them to me.

[Kim looks at Jamal, who shakes his head.]

TOMMY: Come on!

JAMAL: We have to talk, Tommy . . .

TOMMY: Enough talk! I want my keys back!

[Tommy lunges at Kim. She steps back and Tommy falls to the sidewalk.]

HANK: Tom, you all right?

TOMMY: *[getting up, embarrassed]* I'm fine, I'm fine. I just slipped.

KIM: *[to Hank]* Now do you still think he's sober enough to drive?

HANK: Uh, Tommy, maybe we should go back to Dave's and have some black coffee.

TOMMY: I don't believe this! Even my best friend is turning on me! I've driven after drinking twice as much as I did tonight, and I've *never* had an accident.

JAMAL: Maybe you were just lucky. I was in an accident a year ago with my older cousin; remember? He thought he could drive with a lot of beer, too. But he smashed into a tree. It was just luck that we both weren't killed or hurt badly. I don't want to push my luck again, Tom.

TOMMY: I'm sorry about that, Jamal, but I'm fine, and I don't need any coffee. Now give me the keys, Kim, and let's get going.

[Kim looks at Tommy for a moment and then hands the keys to Jamal.]

JAMAL: What's this?

KIM: I had a friend who was killed by a drunken driver. You drive, Jamal.

TOMMY: Are you kidding? He doesn't even have his license! Not one of you does except for me!

KIM: No, but Jamal can drive, and he only had one beer all night.

TOMMY: Sure, he drives. His old man just taught him. But my car's a standard. Your dad's car is an automatic. Right, Jamal?

JAMAL: That's right.

LISA: Can you drive a standard, Jamal?

JAMAL: I think I can.

LISA: What do you mean *think*?

KIM: Don't worry. Tommy can show him how to shift.

TOMMY: Not in this life! He's not getting near my steering wheel. Give me the keys, Jamal.

HANK: Tommy, take it easy. You're getting angry over nothing.

TOMMY: If you're my friend, Hank, you should be on my side, not *theirs*!

HANK: I *am* on your side, but I think we should stay calm and talk this out.

TOMMY: There's nothing more to talk about. Jamal isn't driving my car. He'd drive it into a tree before we got to the next block.

JAMAL: And you wouldn't in the shape you're in?

TOMMY: Why, you lousy—

[Tommy swings at Jamal. They start to fight. The keys fall from Jamal's hand. Tommy goes for them, but Lisa snatches them up.]

LISA: Look, this has gone on long enough. It's cold out here, and we've all got to get home.

TOMMY: So give me the keys, and I'll get you home.

LISA: You're too drunk to drive, Tommy. I'm not sure Jamal should drive either. I think you should go back to Dave's and call home. Your dad can pick us up in his car and drive us home. You can get your car in the morning.

TOMMY: That's the dumbest idea I've heard yet! My old man would have a fit if he knew I'd been drinking. He'd ground me for a month! I'd rather walk home!

LISA: Then we'll have to call someone else's parents. Who wants to call their mom or dad?

[No one speaks.]

LISA: Nobody wants to get in trouble for drinking, right?

JAMAL: You got it.

LISA: I guess that includes me.

HANK: Well, we've got to do something! We can't just stand around here arguing all night.

TOMMY: Look, I'll drive super slow. I'll even stop at every stop sign. How about it, Lisa?

LISA: Well, that sounds more reasonable . . .

KIM: I don't know. I don't think it's safe for Tommy to drive at *any* speed.

JAMAL: She's right. You can have an accident driving too slow just as easily as driving too fast.

HANK: So what are we going to do?

LISA: I think we should put it to a vote.

JAMAL: Yeah. The majority rules. What do you say, Tommy?

TOMMY: I think you're nuts.

HANK: It sounds fair to me. Come on, Tom.

TOMMY: OK! OK! I'll go along with the majority.

LISA: All right. Who votes for Tommy driving us home?
[Tommy and Lisa put up their hands.]

LISA: And who thinks Jamal should drive Tommy's car?
[Jamal and Kim put up their hands.]

TOMMY: Hank, you didn't vote!

JAMAL: Come on, Hank. You can break the tie.

TOMMY: That's right, pal.

KIM: Before you vote, Hank, remember that we're your friends as much as Tommy is. You're not going to put all our lives in danger, are you?

LISA: Don't listen to her, Hank. Better Tommy driving a little drunk than Jamal driving a car he has no experience with.
[Hank looks around at his friends. He takes the car keys from Lisa.]

HANK: I vote that . . .

1. Why do you think his friends decided that Tommy might be too drunk to drive?

2. Are Lisa's reasons for changing her mind about Tommy's driving reasonable? Why or why not?

3. If you were Tommy's father, would you be angrier with him for driving drunk or for calling you to pick him up? Give reasons for your answer.

4. How else could people in this situation get home other than in ways the characters have considered?

5. Do you think Hank would be a better friend to Tommy if he voted to let him drive or not to drive? Explain your answer.

IIIII *THINKING ABOUT THE ENDING*

Think about what has happened in the play up to this point. Do you think Hank will vote for Tommy to drive or for Jamal to drive? Or will he come up with a third alternative? What would be the safest way out of this situation?

Write an ending for the play using what you know about the characters to predict how the play should be resolved. Make sure you include the other characters' reactions to Hank's decision.

The Dreaming Tree

by Kipp Erante Cheng

Characters:
Jeffrey
Mrs. Apple

Scene: *a bench at a bus station in the city. Mrs. Apple is seated on the bench, surrounded by her bags. Jeffrey enters and sits next to Mrs. Apple. She looks at him for a moment.*

MRS. APPLE: Hello there, young man.

JEFFREY: Hello, ma'am.

MRS. APPLE: You don't have to call me *ma'am*. You can call me by my name. *[extending her hand to Jeffrey]* I'm Mrs. Apple.

JEFFREY: Hi. I'm Jeffrey.

[They shake hands.]

MRS. APPLE: Good to meet you, Jeffrey. Where are you going?

JEFFREY: I don't really know. I might go visit a friend in Des Moines.

MRS. APPLE: I'm getting onto a bus that will take me to the country. When I get there, I'll be reunited with my son. I haven't seen him in nearly 20 years.

JEFFREY: That's a long time not to see your son. How come you haven't seen him in such a long time?

MRS. APPLE: When he was a young man, we got into a fight, and we never saw each other again.

JEFFREY: That must have been some fight.

MRS. APPLE: It was. About 20 years ago. My son—his name is Harold—wanted to move away from the city and . . . I'm probably boring you with my story. A young boy like you probably doesn't want to hear the stories of an old lady.

JEFFREY: No, I'd really like to hear about your son.

MRS. APPLE: Harold wanted to move to the country and start a farm, but I told him that I thought he wouldn't be able to succeed because he had never worked on a farm before. So he went anyway, and I didn't hear from him again until he wrote a letter asking me to come and visit him and his wife and children. *[takes out a photograph]* This is my family.

JEFFREY: That's a nice cow.

MRS. APPLE: *[laughing]* Yes. They have a lot of different animals on their farm. That's my grandson standing next to his mother. That's my son Harold standing with my granddaughter.

JEFFREY: They look like nice people.

MRS. APPLE: I think they're very nice people. I'm looking forward to seeing them.

JEFFREY: You're lucky. I mean, you have a family that you can turn to.

MRS. APPLE: Well, Jeffrey, it wasn't always that way. Where are your parents?

JEFFREY: They're at home.

MRS. APPLE: I don't want to sound nosy, but . . .

JEFFREY: No, you're not being nosy.

MRS. APPLE: Are you running away from home?

JEFFREY: Well, no. Not really. I have that friend I might visit. Besides, I don't really have a home to run away from.

MRS. APPLE: What about where your parents live? That's your home, isn't it?

JEFFREY: It used to be. But then my mother had a new baby, and everything at home changed. Now, all my parents do is get on my case. They're always telling me that my room is a mess, and I dress like a slob, and I play my music too loudly.

MRS. APPLE: All teenagers go through those kinds of problems with their parents.

JEFFREY: It seems as if all I ever do is fight with them. They are constantly nagging me about getting better grades at school and working harder so that I can get into a good college. But what if I don't want to go to college? What if I want to play with my rock band?

MRS. APPLE: I'm sure your parents want what is best for you.

JEFFREY: I doubt it. We got into this major fight today, and I told them that I was just going to run away, and you know what they said to me?

MRS. APPLE: What did they say?

JEFFREY: They said, "Good riddance!" Can you believe that? I'm their son, and they said they would be happier without me. So that's why I left. I don't need to take that from them.

MRS. APPLE: I'm sure your parents didn't mean it. I'm sure they're worried about you right now.

JEFFREY: They're probably happy that they can change my bedroom into the baby's new room. It's so unfair. I was the first kid in the house, and my parents used to let me keep my room as messy as I wanted. Now I always have to pick things up in case the baby gets to my stuff. It's always baby this and baby that. It's like they're totally obsessed. They've forgotten about me.

MRS. APPLE: Have you talked to your parents about your feelings?

JEFFREY: They don't really have time to listen.

MRS. APPLE: I wish I had taken time to listen to my son, way back when. We wouldn't have gotten into our big fight. If I could do it all over again, I would try to listen to him more.

JEFFREY: Really?

MRS. APPLE: A lot of the time, parents don't really understand what their children need from them. Not until it's too late.

JEFFREY: You think so?

MRS. APPLE: Yes. I don't want you to make the mistake of not giving your parents a chance. You should talk to them and let them know how you feel.

JEFFREY: My parents don't understand me. They just want to hassle me because they have nothing better to do. I can't spend my entire life studying or cleaning my room. I have things to do.

MRS. APPLE: What do you have to do?

JEFFREY: I don't know. Play video games, watch TV, practice with my band. I have lots of things to do.

MRS. APPLE: Then you should make a deal with your parents. You should tell them that if you keep your room clean and do your homework, then you should be allowed to play video games and everything you like to do.

JEFFREY: It's already too late. My parents are happy that I ran away.

MRS. APPLE: Are you sure about that?

JEFFREY: They said so. Besides, what about my pride? They said they didn't want me. I can't go back home and apologize. I want my parents to come to me and tell me that they were wrong—

MRS. APPLE: Such a stubborn young boy. Just like my own son . . .

JEFFREY: I'm almost 14. In some countries, I would be considered a man. When I was a kid—

MRS. APPLE: You're still a kid. Don't try to grow up so quickly.

JEFFREY: When I was a younger kid, my father told me a story about the dreaming tree. It was a huge tree, maybe a giant oak or something like that, somewhere in the country. When my father was young, he used to go to this tree and tell all of his wishes and dreams to this tree, and they would all come true.

MRS. APPLE: Sounds like a powerful tree.

JEFFREY: I know that it's just a story, and I don't believe in the fairy tales that my parents used to tell me when I was younger, but sometimes I wish there was such a thing as the dreaming tree. I mean, I wish there was a way my dreams could come true . . .

MRS. APPLE: Maybe the dreaming tree isn't a fairy tale like you think it is.

JEFFREY: What do you mean?

MRS. APPLE: I don't know. If you wish hard enough, sometimes things come true. I always wished that I would see my son again, and now I'm going to see him.

JEFFREY: You're lucky.

MRS. APPLE: I have an idea. What if you call your parents and tell them where you are? Maybe they would be willing to allow you to come to the country with me. It would be like a little vacation. And afterward, you could go back home and be with your family again.

JEFFREY: I don't think my parents care what I do. If I call them now, I'll look stupid.

MRS. APPLE: Come on, Jeffrey. I think you should call your parents. They're probably worried about you right now.

JEFFREY: Maybe. And maybe not. Remember: They told me to leave. What if I just go with you and forget about calling? Or if you don't want me to do that, I can do what I was going to do and go visit my friend.

MRS. APPLE: Here's a quarter. Make the phone call, Jeffrey.

[Jeffrey considers the quarter for a moment.]

MRS. APPLE: Go on. What are you waiting for?

[Jeffrey gets up from the bench.]

JEFFREY: Mrs. Apple, I think—

IIII■*THINKING ABOUT THE PLAY*

1. Why does Jeffrey believe that running away will solve his problems?

2. What do Mrs. Apple and Jeffrey have in common?

3. Why do you think Mrs. Apple is willing to take Jeffrey with her to her son's house?

4. What prevents Jeffrey from calling his parents and telling them where he is?

5. Do you think Jeffrey should go to the country with Mrs. Apple? Why or why not?

Jeffrey runs away from home because he has problems with the way that his parents have treated him. When he meets Mrs. Apple and learns about her conflict with her son, he discovers that running away doesn't always solve problems. However, he is torn between his sense of pride and his need for family.

Write an ending that explains what Jeffrey decides. Does Jeffrey swallow his pride and call his parents, or does he run away? If he runs away, where does he go? Include how his parents and Mrs. Apple react to his decision.

Moira Gallagher, Seminole

by Joyce Haines

Characters:
Moira Gallagher
Eileen Gallagher
Sally
Patricia
Madeline
Samantha

Scene One: *the living room of the Gallaghers' new mansion in suburban Philadelphia. At one end of the large room, Moira and Sally are speaking intensely as they look out toward the swimming pool. Moira is wearing a simple gray dress and high heels. Her black hair is in a bun. At the other end, Eileen, Patricia, Madeline, and Samantha chat as they play bridge.*

PATRICIA: *[in a low voice]* Eileen, you should be proud of what you've done for Moira.

EILEEN: *[proudly]* She's received the best education money could buy. She speaks French fluently, plays the violin like an angel, and she's a champion swimmer. We built the pool so that she can practice every day. But most important, she's a wonderful person.

MADELINE: *[whispering]* What advice did the adoption agency give you?

EILEEN: They reminded us to tell her how special she is—as if we had to be told that. They suggested we say *chosen* whenever we mention the adoption and not tell her things that might confuse her. We haven't told her anything except that she's special because we chose her and that our family is very lucky to be together.

SAMANTHA: What a happy ending. I wonder what happened to her real parents. Do you have any . . .

EILEEN: *[drawing back and speaking sharply] We* are her real parents. Michael and I have raised her.

SAMANTHA: Oh, I didn't mean to hurt your feelings, Eileen. Of course you're her real mother.

EILEEN: I guess I'm a little sensitive on that point. Let's finish the game and then move to the terrace for dessert.

MOIRA: *[whispering]* You're right, Sally. Eileen and Michael are good parents. They never wanted to hurt me. I know they love me—they've been so good to me. And they always bought me anything I ever wanted.

SALLY: As Eileen puts it, *[speaking in a high, false voice]* "My Moira has her own private library of the classics in leather bindings with gold titles. Of course, they're not just for looks. She's read *every* one of them."

MOIRA: *[smiles, and then joins Sally in imitating Eileen]* "The only book your great-grandparents had back in Ireland was the family Bible. But it had enough extra pages to record our family history back to the 17th century. They didn't have the luxuries we have today, sweetheart. You don't know just how lucky you are." *[Sally and Moira burst into laughter.]*

EILEEN: What's so funny over there, girls? *[She continues without waiting for an answer.]* Come join us for dessert.

MOIRA: We'll be right there, Mo—*[then stops abruptly and whispers to Sally]* It doesn't feel right to call her *mother* now that I know where my *real* mother came from. I wish Eileen had given me some details about the adoption. She always looked so scared and confused whenever I asked about my real mother. If you hadn't gotten a copy of my birth certificate, I wouldn't even know that she was . . . I mean . . . is . . . Seminole.

SALLY: Oh, Moira.

MOIRA: Sally, you don't know what it feels like to be an outsider. To you, looking up a family tree is just a hobby. I've always felt like an alien in my own family. Can you imagine our family reunions? Eight aunts, 7 uncles, and 16 cousins—all with red hair and blue eyes. Every year, Uncle John points at me and says the same thing: "Well, this one won't get lost in a crowd; that's for sure!"

SALLY: Come on, Moira. Nobody likes family reunions—and we all hate our families. It's only natural.

MOIRA: It's just not the same for me. I don't want to hate my family. Ever since I can remember, I've had questions that I couldn't ask Eileen. Why was I adopted in the first place? What happened to my *real* mother and father? Where are they now? What's my real name?

SALLY: Well, *I* can't answer all of those questions, even if I did get an A on my genealogy research paper. Let's go over what we know. Maybe some of the pieces will fit together.

MOIRA: OK.

SALLY: According to the birth certificate, your real mother came from St. Augustine, Florida. She was—*is*—a full-blooded member of the Seminole nation. Your father's background is listed as *other*. That's not much to go on, with their names blacked out. The adoption was handled 16 years ago by the Chrysalis Agency.

MOIRA: *[desperately]* But why wasn't I given to my grand-parents if my parents couldn't keep me? What does *other* mean? I wonder what part of me is Seminole. I must have inherited something from my mother. I wonder what it's like to live on the Seminole reservation.

SALLY: Think, Moira. You must have overheard Eileen and Michael talking about this at least once in all these years.

MOIRA: I remember watching an after-school television program with Mademoiselle Renée. I was about 7 at the time because I still needed a baby-sitter while Mo—I mean Eileen—was at the factory. Mademoiselle Renée insisted that we watch educational TV together so that she could improve her English. The program showed two Seminole women. It was the first time I ever saw anyone who looked like me. They were so beautiful, with their long skirts and blouses with colorful ribbons. That night, I begged Eileen to take me to Florida. It was one of the only times she ever said no. I'll never forget the worried look on her face.

SALLY: Do you think Eileen knew something bad about your Seminole mother?

MOIRA: Maybe. Or maybe she was just afraid that I would run away to go live with my *real* family. I wish I knew.

Scene Two: Moira's bedroom, three months later. The bed is covered with library books about Native Americans. Moira is wearing a loose cotton blouse with colorful embroidery. Her long hair is flowing past her shoulders. Sally is jiggling her car keys and looking at her watch as Moira sorts through the books.

MOIRA: Classes at Bryn Mawr start in two months. Eileen's so excited that I'm getting the education she never had. She just told me about my graduation present. We're going to Ireland to visit the relatives she's never seen. She's at the travel agency right now. I wish I could tell her that I'd rather visit my real home in Florida. You know, see my *real* family . . . my *nation*, before I begin college.

SALLY: Do you want to drive down there together? I'd love to go with you.

MOIRA: No, thanks for the offer, but if I go, I have to go alone. To tell the truth, I might not want to come back.

SALLY: If you go, what would you tell Eileen?

MOIRA: That's the problem. It would break Eileen's heart.

SALLY: Can you make up a story, like a swim meet?

MOIRA: I'm not sure I could lie to her, especially after all Eileen has done for me. But to meet my *real* family and know my *real* name, Sally. Maybe see the faces of my sisters, cousins, people who look like me. *[She sighs.]* But what if they don't want me? What if they gave me away because they never wanted to see me again?

All this time, no one from there has ever tried to reach me. But maybe they didn't know how to. Oh, I don't know.

SALLY: When would you go?

MOIRA: I haven't made up my mind yet. There's too much at stake. Why risk hurting the only parents I've even known if there's nothing there for me? I'm so confused. I know how they'd feel if I went. They'd never really forgive me. And they're right—they couldn't have loved me more, or given me more.

SALLY: *[waves her arm across the library books]* It looks like you've read everything about Seminoles in the entire Philadelphia library.

MOIRA: *[excited, picking up a book and turning to a page with a bookmark]* Did you know that my nation's name actually came from a Muskogee word that means "emigrant" or "frontiersman"? The Muskogee term came from *cimarrón*—the Spanish word for a tame animal that turns wild again. See?

SALLY: *[pretending interest]* That's fascinating. Come on, we've got to hurry if we want to catch the movie.

MOIRA: Wait. There's more. It says in this book that the Seminoles "welcomed runaway African and Caribbean slaves from Southern plantations. A few Seminoles and former slaves married and raised families." Maybe that explains *other* on my birth certificate.

SALLY: OK, but we still don't have a family name. Why don't you just accept the fact that you're a Gallagher now? It could be a lot worse, you know. You're really lucky. . . .

MOIRA: *[suddenly tense]* I hate that word.

SALLY: I'm sorry, Moira.

MOIRA: I'm sorry, too. I didn't mean to snap at you. It's just that . . .

SALLY: I understand. Let's get going.

MOIRA: If you don't mind, I think I'd rather skip it tonight. I've got a lot on my mind.

Scene Three: *Moira's bedroom, eight days later. Moira and Sally are sitting side by side on the bed.*

SALLY: What was it you wanted to tell me?

MOIRA: It's about my adoption. I've read that some traditional Native Americans believe in waiting four nights before making an important decision—seven nights for a really serious problem.

SALLY: Why do they do that?

MOIRA: They believe the answer might come in a dream. Well, I tried it. I gave myself seven nights to decide whether or not to look for my other family. Last night was the final night. Something wonderful happened.

SALLY: Well, what did your dreams tell you? What have you decided?

MOIRA: I'm going to . . .

IIIII THINKING ABOUT THE PLAY

1. Describe Eileen. Do you think she is a good mother? Why or why not?

2. Was it a good idea or not for Eileen to tell Moira so few details about her adoption? Explain.

3. Why do you think Moira doesn't like the word *lucky*?

4. What reasons could there have been for Moira's adoption by the Gallaghers?

5. What evidence does the play offer that Moira begins to see herself as a Seminole?

IIIII *THINKING ABOUT THE ENDING*

Think about what you learned about Moira's relationship with the woman who raised her. Do you think she will decide to find her birth parents? Is there another way to resolve the play that might be easier on her adoptive parents?

Write your own ending to the play, showing Moira's thoughts and actions as she decides either to search for her birth parents in Florida or spend the summer with Eileen in Ireland.

Kareem's Party

by Wiley M. Woodard

Characters:
Kareem
Luis
Maria

Scene: *evening in the living room of the Sanchez home. Kareem is with Maria Sanchez, waiting for Luis.*

KAREEM: I know it's late. You and Luis are probably getting ready to have dinner. I promise I won't be here long.

MARIA: We won't be having dinner for a while yet. You're welcome to join us, Kareem. We have plenty.

KAREEM: No, thank you, Mrs. Sanchez. My parents are expecting me home for dinner.

MARIA: Can I offer you something to drink?

KAREEM: No, thank you. I'm fine.
[Luis enters in his wheelchair.]

MARIA: Well, I'll leave you two alone.
[Maria exits.]

KAREEM: *Qué pasa, mi amigo?*

LUIS: What's up?

KAREEM: It's been a little while since I've seen you. I just came by to see how you're doing.

LUIS: I'm doing fine.

KAREEM: Well, I wouldn't have known by the way you've been acting lately.

LUIS: What do you mean by that, Kareem?

KAREEM: You barely talk to me after school anymore. Whenever I start a conversation with you, you seem to want to get away from me. And suddenly you don't want to watch the games on TV. I want to know what gives.

LUIS: I've been busy working on a history report.

KAREEM: Do you need any help with it? You know I like history.

LUIS: No thanks, Kareem. I'm managing just fine.

KAREEM: Talk to me. I know you've got more than your history report on your mind. What's going on?

LUIS: Maybe I'm just missing my old neighborhood.

KAREEM: Missing your old neighborhood? You told me how much you wanted to leave there. You told me you couldn't wait to move. Not that this apartment building is the Taj Mahal . . .

LUIS: What I mean is, I'm missing my friends from Vermont Avenue.

KAREEM: Why now? You never seemed to miss them all that much before. And what about me?

LUIS: I'm beginning to think my real friends are the ones from Vermont Avenue.

KAREEM: What do you mean, your *real* friends? Lynn, Dusty, and I—we're your real friends. Besides, I always thought I was your *best* friend.

LUIS: I thought you were my best friend, once.

KAREEM: What do you mean *once*? What're you talking about?

LUIS: *[bitterly]* You want to talk about your birthday party? It seems to me that if I'm your best friend, I wouldn't have to hear about your party from Lynn! Imagine how that made me feel. Everyone is looking forward to your party, and I didn't even know about it.

KAREEM: *[uncomfortably]* I'm sorry about that, Luis. Believe me, I was going to tell you.

LUIS: Right. When? After the party was over?

KAREEM: Uh . . . not exactly.

LUIS: The party is three days away. Everyone knows about it. Up until a few days ago, you and I were watching the basketball playoffs on TV almost every day. In all that time, you didn't breathe one word about your party. *[sarcastically]* I guess you were so caught up in the games it slipped your mind?

KAREEM: Well . . . no.

LUIS: Then why did you keep the whole thing from me?

[Kareem hesitates for a moment.]

KAREEM: Luis, I thought you might be uncomfortable. My parents had already made plans to have the party at The Fun Spot. It's not wheelchair accessible. If my parents changed the place now, they'd lose their deposit. From there, we were going to meet at the park. The girls challenged the guys to a game of volleyball.

LUIS: For me, it's really hard making friends. Most of the kids just stare at me. You know that. I thought none of that mattered to you. I thought you were different.

KAREEM: I *am* different. Believe it or not, Luis, I *was* thinking of you. I thought we would go and do something else to celebrate later.

LUIS: If you were really thinking of me, you would know it hurts to be left out. Are you ashamed of having a friend like me, Kareem?

KAREEM: Not at all. You're like my brother.

LUIS: OK. Let's put it on the line. Are you willing to change your party so I can go?

KAREEM: I . . .

||||■ THINKING ABOUT THE PLAY

1. Do you think Kareem was thinking of Luis's comfort when he didn't tell him about his birthday party plans? Why?

2. Why do you think Kareem planed a party that Luis couldn't participate in?

3. How does Luis's disability affect his friendship with Kareem?

4. Write three adjectives that describe Kareem and three that describe Luis.

5. Do you think the discussion between the two characters will change their relationship? Explain.

||||■THINKING ABOUT THE ENDING

Think about what you learned about Kareem and Luis. Do you think Kareem will apologize to Luis and invite him to his party? Why or why not?

Write an ending for the play in which you use what you know about Kareem and Luis to predict what they will do and how they will deal with their feelings about Kareem's party.

A Friendship Offered

by James Bruchac

Characters:
Eddy
Dane
Trip

Scene: *ten minutes after school is let out, in front of Central High School. Eddy is sitting on a bench waiting for friends to pick him up. As he sits, Dane approaches him.*

DANE: Hey, Eddy, what's up? *[sitting next to Eddy]*

EDDY: *[turning his head toward Dane]* Nothing much. Just waiting for some of my friends to pick me up.

DANE: So, how are things with you? I haven't talked much to you since we ran track last season.

EDDY: Things are real good. Everything is coming together for me.

DANE: Track starts in another month. Are you ready to take the title away from me this year? You really gave me a run for my money at the state championships last year.

EDDY: Some friends and I have some plans. Track just takes up too much time. There are people to see, and there's money to be made. *[holding his wallet up to Dane]*

DANE: You're not running this year? You're one of the best runners in the state. You can't give that up.

EDDY: It's time I started thinking about my future. Besides, the track team already has its state champion.

DANE: Thanks to you. You're half the reason I won.

EDDY: How's that?

DANE: You know what I mean. Every day in practice, we pushed each other. You were always on my heels.

EDDY: Did Coach Sherman put you up to this? I know he's been asking why I'm not around.

DANE: No, I was just curious why you hadn't called up to train with me in the off season. I had no idea that—

EDDY: That what? I don't have time anymore for some stupid sport. I could be doing better things.

DANE: You never would have said this last year, Eddy.

EDDY: I got smart. While I was busting my tail in school and track, I could have been making money. My friends, they're the ones that helped me see that.

DANE: Which friends would those be?

EDDY: Trip and Bud. Some guys from the neighborhood.

DANE: Didn't Trip drop out of school two years ago?

EDDY: That's right. Trip dropped out of school, and it was the best decision he ever made.

DANE: How's that?

EDDY: After his father ran off, someone had to pay the bills. Now he's got a real good business going. Bud's his partner, and they both asked me to come work for them.

DANE: You're thinking of dropping out of school?

EDDY: That's right. I've wasted too much of my time already. Starting next week, I'm going into business with my friends. They've got money, and they didn't make it sitting in class all day and running after school.

DANE: They may have the money, but they'll never have what you've got.

EDDY: Oh yeah? What's that?

DANE: A chance at making it in track and school. You're a great athlete, and your grades—they're not that bad. Those guys, Trip and Bud—they probably never had that. Besides, it sounds like Trip didn't have much choice.

EDDY: Man, why do you care?

DANE: I know what you could be if you stick with it.

EDDY: What do you think I could be? *[sarcastically]* Like you?

DANE: Maybe. Maybe better. I'm two years ahead of you. You've already broken all my old records. After I graduate, you've got a good chance at the state championships. That is, if you don't take it away from me this year.

EDDY: Well, you don't have to worry about that. What can that get me, anyway? A plastic trophy? I'll be able to buy a million of those a year from now.

DANE: Victories like that come from the heart. You know money can't buy you that.

EDDY: *[angrily]* So now you're going to throw some of your native mumbo-jumbo philosophy at me to try and make me guilty? Forget it. It won't work.

DANE: It's not mumbo jumbo, and you should respect your own culture.

EDDY: How's it my culture? No one ever taught me any of

that stuff. All I know about being Native American is from what I see on TV.

DANE: You think I was taught about it as a kid? No. That doesn't matter. You can learn it yourself.

EDDY: You're Cherokee. I'm Abenaki. We're not even from the same nation.

DANE: That doesn't matter. Even if you weren't Native American, you're a human being. I know we share that.

EDDY: So? Why do you care what I do?

DANE: OK, part of it *is* because we're both Native American. But it's also because you could really be somebody. I just don't want you to make a big mistake.

EDDY: You never cared last year when we trained together. You were all wrapped up in your future—your big college scholarship, your big, important friends.

DANE: You're right. I didn't seem to care much back then, but I've been thinking differently lately.

EDDY: Oh yeah? How come?

DANE: I'm not sure, exactly. Maybe the stuff I've been reading about my people has helped. Or maybe it's just the fact that I've gotten my scholarship, and I feel like helping someone else.

EDDY: No one like you has ever wanted to help me in the past. Why do I need it now?

DANE: People need someone who cares about what they do in life.

EDDY: So all of a sudden, after three years of competition, when you did everything you could to beat me, you want to help me?

DANE: It sounds crazy, but it's true. I just want to help.

EDDY: It does sound crazy. Even if you're for real, who says I need your help—or anyone's help? From my point of view, I'm making the best decision.

DANE: How can giving up be a good decision?

EDDY: I'm not giving up, I'm just trying to make it. Look at Walter Johnson. He stayed in school, even got a football scholarship to Penn State. A year later, he failed out. Now he's back in the projects living with his mom.

DANE: No one ever said it was easy, but at least he tried.

EDDY: He tried all right. Tried and failed. Trip's business is the best chance I have at a sure thing. I'll even be able to afford an apartment with Bud. I'm tired of waiting.

DANE: Did you tell your parents?

EDDY: Man, they don't care. They're just happy to get me out of the house. They've got their own problems anyway, always yelling and screaming at each other. I don't even know why they're still together.

DANE: My family life at home isn't much better, Eddy. Two years ago, I felt just like you. I almost made the same mistake.

EDDY: What?

DANE: Giving up on myself, giving up on school—the whole bit.

EDDY: Well, what happened?

DANE: Coach Sherman. He talked me out of it. He saw I was feeling down during practice one day, so he pulled me over and talked with me. After finding out how much we had in common, I listened to his advice.

EDDY: *[slightly aggravated]* So, Coach Sherman *did* put you up to this!

DANE: No, man, I swear, this was all my idea, like I said. But Coach did motivate me in another way.

EDDY: How?

DANE: I know this sounds dumb, but he really did care. I've been thinking a lot lately about what he did for me. I want to do the same thing for someone else.

EDDY: Listen, Dane. I understand you may really want to help. But, like I said, I'm making the best choice. Besides, Trip and Bud have always been good friends to me. We grew up watching each other's backs. Now they're offering to get me in on a real sweet deal.

DANE: Trip isn't like you and me.

EDDY: In what way? Not being Native American?

DANE: No. Trip was forced to make a decision. He had to help support his family; that's why he quit. Even if he'd stayed in school, he wasn't college material, like us.

EDDY: So what if I do make it to college? Like I said before, I could just be the next Walter Johnson. At least, if I quit now, I'll have a head start on life instead of failing out and having nothing.

DANE: You can't think that way, man. Nothing is 100 percent, but that shouldn't stop you from trying. You should at least finish high school. I know you can do that. Anyway, if Trip and Bud have such a good business, it should still be around in a couple of years. Right?

EDDY: Yeah, and maybe then they won't want me.

DANE: Take it step by step. You haven't failed yet. Why quit? And if you do fail and can't go on anymore, I'm sure your friends would still give you a job.

EDDY: Like I said, maybe yes and maybe no. All right, so what if I did decide to stay in school this year? What about next year? You'll be off at college. Are you telling me you're going to care then?

DANE: I'll be back, Eddy, and you could always call me at school if you need to talk.

[At that moment, Eddy's friend Trip drives up.]

TRIP: *[leaning his head out the car window]* Hey, Eddy, you coming or what? Bud found a real nice apartment!

DANE: What's it going to be, Eddy?

TRIP: Come on, Eddy; we've got an appointment to meet with the landlord! Hurry up!

DANE: It's all up to you, man.

EDDY: *[looking back and forth between the car and Dane as he stands up]* I think . . .

1. What is Eddy and Dane's relationship like? List two things they have in common.

2. Why does Eddy mistrust Dane?

3. Do you believe Dane honestly wants to help Eddy, or did the coach just put him up to it? Explain.

4. How important are Trip and Bud to Dane?

5. What do you think will happen to Eddy's friendship with Trip and Bud if he doesn't take their offer?

||||| THINKING ABOUT THE ENDING

Consider Dane and Eddy's conversation and their relationship. Eddy has made up his mind to leave school; then Dane tries to talk him out of it. What are the advantages of leaving? What are the disadvantages?

Using what you know about Eddy from the play, write an ending in which he decides whether to follow Dane's advice or not. Include Dane's reaction and the reaction of Eddy's friends.

The Boy With No Clothes

by Brenda Lane Richardson

Characters:
Tyrone
Bobbie

Scene: *Tyrone's bedroom. Fifteen-year-old Tyrone enters his room dressed in a bathrobe, drying his neck with a towel. He is obviously delighted with himself.*

TYRONE: *[reading aloud, in a high voice, from a letter received at school]* "Ty, you asked me to let you know if Reggie and I ever broke up. Well, I'm letting you know. Reggie is history. Now, you're the man. Meet me tonight in front of the Shoreline. My friends and I'll be outside at 8:00. Yours, Cookie." *[folding the letter and kissing it.]* Yes, I am the man. *[staring into the mirror and speaking in a baritone]* Cookie, you're so sweet I'd like to eat the words that come from your mouth. *[Humming, he crosses to his closet and opens the door and then looks stunned.]* Where are my clothes! *[Reaching in, he pulls out two sports jackets, dress slacks, V-necked sweaters, button-down shirts, several ties, and three suits. Racing to a dresser drawer, he finds them empty and lets out an angry scream. He begins talking to himself again.]* Calm down, it's going to be all right. This a dream. My clothes will be where they're supposed to be when I wake up. *[racing to the mirror and slapping himself]* But if this is a nightmare, how come I felt that?

[A door can be heard slamming from afar, and someone races up the stairs. Bobbie stands in the doorway, a smirk on her face.]

BOBBIE: Guess I don't have to tell you Daddy's home.

TYRONE: Is he crazy?

BOBBIE: Bet you won't ask him that.

TYRONE: What am I going to do?

BOBBIE: He said he's been telling you about dressing like a bum. *[in a monotone voice, as if their father has delivered this speech so often, she has it memorized]* He said he works too hard and has sacrificed too much to keep us in this house, to put us in the best schools, to . . .

[Tyrone joins in.]

TYRONE AND BOBBIE: . . . scrimp and save so that one day we could go to college and live the kind of life he never got to live, and that his father never even dreamed of, so we can, along with all the young people of this world, inherit the earth.

BOBBIE: And today, he also said . . .

TYRONE: Oh, put a lid on it. I know what he said. Every time he comes back from one of his business trips, he gives me another lecture.

BOBBIE: It's not really another lecture. This time he's not lecturing, he's doing. *[Lifting one of the new shirts and wearing it draped across her head, she prances like a runway model.]* Daddy brought these all the way from France. You'd fit right in in Paris.

TYRONE: I need to look cool, not like a walking geography

lesson. How am I going to go out on the street in these? I'll be run out of town.

BOBBIE: If I had to choose between being disgraced and having to tell Daddy that I wouldn't wear these clothes, I . . .

TYRONE: [*a sudden gleam in his eyes*] Maybe I won't have to explain anything. Where is he, anyway?

BOBBIE: He went to the hospital to find Mom. She doesn't know he's back. He's taking us all out to some fancy new restaurant, and he expects you to be here and dressed when he gets back.

TYRONE: I'm busy tonight.

BOBBIE: You're right about that, but not busy the way you want to be. Dad's really excited about some new deal. He wants to celebrate with all of us. Even if he has to sit and wait until Mom comes out of surgery, he said he's bringing her home with him.

TYRONE: *[muttering]* I wish she'd operate on him, give him a new brain. *[grinning]* But it will take him a while to get back . . .

BOBBIE: You're the one who's going to need the new brain if you're thinking what I think you're thinking.

TYRONE: Come on, Sis, help me out here. Where did he put my old clothes? Say, how about we hang together tomorrow?

BOBBIE: *[pulling back]* No, thanks. I don't want Dad to think I'm your partner in crime. I just know you aren't thinking of getting your old clothes from the pile in the basemen—*[slapping her hand over her mouth]* oops!

[Tyrone races out. His voice can be heard as he moves down the stairs.]

TYRONE: Thanks, Sis.

BOBBIE: *[Walking toward the mirror, she talks as if explaining to her father.]* At first, I refused to tell him anything. He tried bribing me. He yelled and screamed. He even threw me down on the floor *[flinging herself to the floor and pretending she's in a fierce battle]* and then he put his hands around my neck. He squeezed tighter and tighter. But even then I didn't give in. *[pretending to sob]* It wasn't until he said he'd tell the kids about that time at the beach, when my bathing suit . . .

[Tyrone appears in the doorway dressed in his old wardrobe.]

TYRONE: *[holding out a paper sack and stuffing clothes from the floor into it]* All I have to do is put these on before I walk back in. *[walking to the mirror and admiring himself]* Now, I am in my power. Cookie, I hope you're ready to greet the king. *[He roars like a lion, while downstairs, a door opens.]*

BOBBIE: Mr. Lion, I think your trainer just arrived. I'm out of here. *[She quickly leaves the room when she hears heavy footsteps moving up the stairs.]*

TYRONE: Dad?

|||||| THINKING ABOUT THE PLAY

1. Do you think Tyrone was dishonest for planning to sneak back into the clothes his father had chosen for him just before returning home? Why?
2. What do you know about Tyrone's father from the play? What do you know about Tyrone?
3. Was Tyrone's dad being fair to him? Why?
4. How might Tyrone have convinced his father that he couldn't wear the new clothes outside?
5. Can you think of any way that Tyrone could have made both himself and his father happy?

|||||| THINKING ABOUT THE ENDING

Think about what you have learned about Tyrone and his father. Do you think that Tyrone will be honest with his dad about what he's doing? Why or why not? Does Tyrone lie to his father about why he's wearing his old clothes, or does he try explaining to his father why he can't wear his new ones? Does Tyrone's father understand or refuse to change his mind?

Write an ending for the play in which you use what you learned about the characters, describing Tyrone's and his father's thoughts and actions.

The Bus Station

by Brenda Lane Richardson

Characters:
Hilton Smith
Mother
Ray

Scene: *The year is 1975. Eighteen-year-old Hilton and his mother enter a Greyhound bus station in Detroit, Michigan, and begin their good-byes. His mother is stern but loving as she hands Hilton a paper sack.*

MOTHER: I fixed all of your favorites, chicken and deviled eggs, and there's some of that lemon cake.

HILTON: *[looking sad]* Thanks, Ma.

MOTHER: Except for this ticket, you won't have a thing other than those few dollars in your pocket. *[pausing]* I would tell you to call me if you have any problems. But the truth is, if you do have any problems, I can't help you anymore, son. You understand that, don't you?

HILTON: *[slightly annoyed]* Stop worrying. I told you, there aren't going to be any more problems. Try to forget about all that's happened.

MOTHER: *[laughing shortly]* Forget. Tell me how to forget that gang you've been in, all the lies and disappointments, and how about your brother, Mr. Big Shot, up there in jail. Should I forget that every penny we could beg and borrow went for your lawyer and that there wasn't any left to get a good lawyer for your brother? I never thought I'd have to choose between my sons. Should I forget that, too?

HILTON: I know you can't forget all that. I think about it every minute. But try to start thinking about the good news you'll be hearing about me. No more lying or stealing. I'm going to go to night school, get a job, and save some money. I'll get him out, Ma, I promise. I'm gonna find a way to make some quick, honest money.

MOTHER: *[bitterly]* And maybe a fairy godmother will leave it under your pillow. *[pausing]* As God's my witness, I want nothing but good for you. But this time, you're on your own. Just remember that temptation can sneak up on you. It's like being punched in the stomach by a ghost. You turn around to see what's hit you, and before you know it, you're flat on your back. You never saw it coming.

HILTON: Not this time. When I went over to the jail yesterday, I took an oath with Danny. I swore to him I'd turn my life around. You'll see, Ma. Just you watch. Give me some time.

MOTHER: *[glancing at her watch]* I didn't notice the time. Miss Grace is hard on me if I'm late. *[hesitating]* I hate to leave you here waiting alone. . . .

HILTON: *[smiling]* Ma, how are you gonna send me off to my new life and act afraid to leave me alone in the bus station?

[They embrace. His mother leaves, and Hilton sits on a bench, clutching his bag and tattered suitcase. After a few minutes, a young Asian boy and his parents, speaking in Vietnamese, crowd onto the bench with Hilton. The boy carefully rests the paper bag he is carrying beside his feet and glances at Hilton, smiling.]

RAY: Your bus stations are wonderful.

HILTON: *[with surprise]* They are?

RAY: *[holding up a paperback book]* Excuse me, I was trying out my English language.

HILTON: I suppose that means you aren't from around here.

RAY: We are from Vietnam, but we want to become Americans. We are going to Minn-e-so-ta.

HILTON: Minnesota. Yeah, man, *[nodding in agreement]* I've heard of it. It's cold. *[pointing at the young man's thin coat]* Sure you're ready for that?

RAY: We will buy coats and—how you say—boots *[Hilton nods his head.]* when we arrive. We could take very little with us, *[nodding toward the floor]* just what we grab up.

HILTON: Yeah, man. I know the feeling. I've got to get out of Dodge myself.

RAY: Is Dodge like Vietnam, where the Communists take over?

HILTON: Not the same, but just as hard.

RAY: It's hard, is it not, to leave those you love?

HILTON: Tell me about it, man.

RAY: My grandfather was too old to come. He was Chinese man, came to Vietnam as a boy with nothing. He build up a jewelry business. Big, big . . .

HILTON: I can dig that.

RAY: But the people, many people, don't like him and us because we are Chinese in Vietnam.

HILTON: Yeah, kind of like here, for black folks.

RAY: My whole family work hard for my grandfather, building business. We have a house, big, big, and we live together. Then, after American soldiers leave Vietnam,

Communists come to our house. They march in, no knock. Beat my grandfather. . . . *[Holding his eyes, he pauses for a minute, wrestling with the memory.]* The rest of us escape. We take a boat to escape. Only things we have are what we grab up. But gold and silver mean nothing when you think of family. On the boat, I look back, see the end of Vietnam for me, end for my sister, end of being a boy. Now, I care for my family.

HILTON: Wow, man. You've had some life. But it's going to get better for both of us. People like the Chinese here. *[laughing]* Hey, at least you'll be treated better than I am. *[Rummaging through his paper sack, Hilton pulls out several slices of his mother's cake and offers them to Ray and Ray's parents. They all take some, thanking Hilton in broken English. Hilton places his sack on the floor near his feet. Soon, an announcer calls.]*

ANNOUNCER: Last call for the 9:30 bus to St. Paul, Minnesota.
[Ray and his family continue enjoying their cake.]

HILTON: Hey, man, didn't you say Minnesota? That's your bus they're calling. You'd better hurry. *[There's a commotion as Ray alerts his parents that they're about to miss their bus. They jump up from the benches, grab their things, wave good-bye to Hilton, and race off. Hilton shakes his head and speaks aloud to himself.]* And I thought I had it bad . . . *[He opens the paper sack to get out an egg and then looks shocked. He lifts out necklaces of silver and gold.]* Wow! This has got to be worth a fortune. *[suddenly realizing]* I could get that lawyer for my brother. *[He stands, as if shading his eyes, and looks out.]* And there goes the bus to St. Paul. If I reported this, maybe they'd contact the bus driver, let that family know their bag was left here. But what if they can't find them? Then some bus driver would keep all this. *[looking again into the bag, and then up]* It's not like I stole it or something. I didn't ask for this. *[lightly touching his forehead]* What would it be like, to come all the way here from Vietnam and not even have money for a coat? At least I have a coat. No, I should look out for my brother. Blood *is* thicker than water, isn't it? *[Hilton stands, deep in thought.]* There's only one thing to do. I'll . . .

||||■THINKING ABOUT THE PLAY

1. Why did Hilton's mother believe it was impossible to forget the past?

2. What did Hilton mean when he told Ray he would probably be treated better in America than Hilton was? Do you agree with him? Why?

3. Why do you think hearing Ray's story made Hilton feel a little better about his own life?

4. Write three adjectives that describe Hilton and three that describe Ray.

5. What argument would you make to Hilton to justify his keeping the jewelry? What argument would you make to convince him to return it?

IIIII THINKING ABOUT THE ENDING

Think about what you have learned about Hilton and the life he has lived up to this point. Do you think he will do whatever is necessary to give back the jewelry, such as contacting a manager in the bus station or calling the station in St. Paul to return the bag? Or do you think Hilton will keep the jewelry, sell it, and try to hire a lawyer who can help his brother?

Write an ending for the play in which you use what you learned about Hilton to predict whether or not he will try to contact Ray and return the jewelry.

The Life of the Party

by Cynthia Benjamin

Characters:
Lee
Sandra
Ken
Nell
Peter
Holly
Larry

Scene One: *the kitchen of Lee's house. Lee is looking in the refrigerator for a snack. His sister Sandra is getting a soft drink. It's 7:00 P.M.*

LEE: You look nice tonight. Where are you guys going?

SANDRA: Mark wants to try the new restaurant on Grant Street.

LEE: Big date, huh?

SANDRA: Come on. Most of the time it's take-out for us. But Mark really aced his midterms. So he wants to celebrate. You know these college types.

LEE: Tell me about them. Remember that guy you went out with two years ago?

SANDRA: *[laughing]* Bobby Frank? What a bozo.

LEE: He was always here for a free meal.

SANDRA: He even showed up at the restaurant once. He wanted dinner on the house. But Dad tossed him out instead. He was drunk out of his mind. *[suddenly embarrassed]*

LEE: That's all right. Don't be embarrassed. Bobby Frank did drink a lot. He was like me. There's one difference. I have a disease. It's called *alcoholism.*

SANDRA: I'm sorry. I guess I said the wrong thing.

LEE: No, you didn't. It's not a big secret or anything. I'm a recovering alcoholic, and I take things day by day.

SANDRA: You've come a long way in just three months.

LEE: Hey, wrapping Dad's car around a tree helped. It was a painful way to get my act together. But the doctors and nurses taught me a few things.

SANDRA: *[smiling]* Like what?

LEE: No beer parties. They're against hospital rules.
[Lee takes an apple and walks slowly to the table. He's limping. Sandra watches him, concerned.]

SANDRA: How's your leg?

LEE: A lot better. I talked to Doctor Ransom today. He said the stiffness will be gone in about six weeks. Hey, I might even be shooting baskets with Dad soon.
[They sit down at the kitchen table.]

SANDRA: You know something? It's nice to have you back. I mean the old you.

LEE: Instead of the drunken clown. Remember? My friends called me the life of the party.

SANDRA: I remember.

LEE: Going to a party was one thing. Staying there was something else. Man, I needed that drink in my hand. Without it, I felt like a major loser. But even my best friends didn't know that.

SANDRA: What about Peter and Ken? Have you talked to them?

LEE: A couple of times since I came home. Peter said there's a party at Ken's house tonight. I guess it's the old crowd.

SANDRA: Why don't you go?

LEE: *[shrugs]* I don't know. I haven't seen them since the night of the accident. *[pointing to his leg]* And until this heals, dancing's out.

SANDRA: So? A lot of the guys won't be dancing. You go to a party to see your friends and hang out.

LEE: And drink. We don't have to pretend the word doesn't exist.

SANDRA: OK. Some of the people at the party will be drinking. And some of them won't. What would you do if you went?

LEE: *[pointing to Sandra's soft drink]* Probably what you're doing. I haven't had any alcohol since the accident. Three months of living sober. I'm not going to screw up now.

SANDRA: *[kissing him]* You know, when you were a little kid, you were always such a pain. What happened?

LEE: I turned into a teenage couch potato. *[getting up from the chair]* Now if you'll excuse me, I'm headed for a night of heavy channel surfing.

SANDRA: They asked you to the party because they wanted to see you again.

LEE: I know.

SANDRA: Mark and I are going out. I know Mom and Dad will be working at the restaurant. It might get a little lonely here.

LEE: I'll let you in on a little secret. When I was boozing, I felt lonelier at parties than I do now by myself. And to tell you the truth, Sandra, it's a little scary for me to think about going. What do I do at a party? How do I act without a drink in my hand?

SANDRA: All the more reason to try a party sober. You might even like it.

Scene Two: *the living room of Ken's house. Music is playing. A party is getting underway. There's a table with food and drinks. As Lee walks in, his friends Ken and Nell come up to welcome him.*

KEN: *[patting Lee on the back]* Hey, man, it's good to see you. Glad you could make it.

NELL: How're you feeling?

LEE: OK. The leg's healing up fine. I'm going back to school next semester.

NELL: Terrific. We've really missed you. I kept meaning to stop by and say hello. But I wasn't sure when you got out of the hospital.

LEE: About six weeks ago.

NELL: I'm sorry. I didn't know it had been so long. *[looking uncomfortable]* I'm going to get something to eat. See you later.

[She walks to another corner of the room. Ken stays with Lee.]

KEN: Sorry about that.

LEE: That's OK. Some people are better at visiting than others. I don't take it personally.

KEN: I really am glad you made it tonight. Peter wasn't sure if you would be here.

LEE: I figured it would be nice to see everyone again. It's been a long time. Say, where is Peter, anyway?

KEN: He just left.

LEE: *[disappointed]* So early?

KEN: *[laughing]* Come on, man. You know Peter better than that. He was here all day helping me set up the sound system.

LEE: *[trying to brighten up]* Remember when we set up the speakers at your party last year?

KEN: Are you kidding? We could have used your expert help this time around.

LEE: Hey, where is he anyway?

[Ken gets a drink from a nearby table. He tries to avoid Lee's question.]

KEN: *[turning to Lee]* Can I get you anything to drink?

LEE: Whatever doesn't have booze in it. *[Ken hands him a soft drink.]* You still haven't told me. Why did Peter split so early?

KEN: He's picking up Holly. She decided to come at the last minute.

LEE: I haven't seen her since we split up. Guess it was just before the accident. *[He gulps down his drink.]* That same night, in fact.

KEN: I'm sorry, man. When Peter invited you, he didn't know she was coming.

LEE: She always did change her mind at the last minute. *[He slaps Ken on the back.]* Hey, forget it. I was bound to run into her when I got back to school. Might as well be tonight. Anyway, I'd like her to know I'm OK.

[Holly and Peter enter the living room. Holly sees Lee talking to Ken.]

KEN: There's something else you should know.

LEE: *[spotting Holly]* Sure. Later, man.
[Lee walks over to Holly and Peter.]

PETER: Glad you came.

LEE: So am I.
[He and Holly stare at each other]

HOLLY: When are you coming back to school?

LEE: Next semester. I saw Mr. Stein last week about my course schedule. If I go to summer school, I should be caught up by the beginning of next year.

HOLLY: I'm glad to hear it.

PETER: I'm going to check on the sound system. *[to Holly]* See you later.
[Holly and Lee look at each other uncomfortably. They both try to talk at the same time.]

HOLLY: When did you leave the—

LEE: My sister said she bumped into you at— *[They look at each other and laugh.]* OK, you first.

HOLLY: I stopped by to visit you in the hospital. But only your family could see you.

LEE: Thanks for trying. My mom told me you had been there. It meant a lot to me.

HOLLY: I'm just so sorry about that accident . . . about everything that happened that night.

LEE: Breaking up with me didn't cause the accident. I did. Of course, I had a lot of help. Six cans of beer made it real easy.

HOLLY: Your sister said you're OK now.

LEE: I've stopped drinking. And there are no hard feelings. *[He looks at Holly for a few seconds.]* In fact, if you have some time, we could go out for coffee. We're still friends, right?

HOLLY: Sure we are, Lee.

PETER: Hey, Holly, did I bring the CDs?

HOLLY: *[to Peter]* You left them in the car. *[She turns to Lee.]* I have to tell you something. It's about Peter and me. *[She stops, embarrassed.]* We've been going together for almost two months.

LEE: Oh. Well. *[trying to sound glad]* I think it's great. Best of luck.

[Lee turns away from Holly. He walks to the refreshment table. Larry walks over.]

LARRY: Hi. My name's Larry. I'm Ken's cousin. *[He picks up a can of beer.]* You look tense, buddy. Have a beer.

LEE: No thanks. I don't drink.

LARRY: Everyone drinks. What harm can a beer do? *[He holds out a can of beer to Lee.]* There's plenty more downstairs. Take it.

[Lee looks at the beer. Then he looks at Holly. She's standing close to Peter, talking to him.]

LEE: Well . . .

IIIII THINKING ABOUT THE PLAY

1. Why do you think Lee's friends called him the life of the party?

2. Why did Lee drink at parties?

3. What does Lee mean when he says, "When I was boozing, I felt lonelier at parties than I do now by myself"?

4. Do you think it was a good idea for Lee to go to the party at Ken's house? Explain your answer.

5. How does Holly feel when she sees Lee at the party? How does Lee feel when he sees her?

IIII THINKING ABOUT THE ENDING

Lee has worked hard to overcome a serious drinking problem. Consider what he has experienced in the past three months. How do you think he feels when he goes to a party and sees his old friends?

Consider what you have learned about Lee and how he's handled his problems in the past. Has he changed? When Larry offers him the beer, what will he do? Write an ending to the play in which he either takes the beer that Larry offers or refuses it.

S tand Up and Be Counted

by Cary Pepper

Characters:
Mike
Joan
Hank
Mr. Zand

Scene: *a neighborhood schoolyard. Mike and Joan meet in the middle.*

MIKE: Thanks for helping me study for tomorrow's test. The library's open until 6:00, so we'll have plenty of time. Meet you here at 3:00?

JOAN: OK. Did you hear about the video store?

MIKE: Yeah! Someone threw paint all over the windows. I saw it on my way to school this morning.

JOAN: Did you hear why?

MIKE: Uh-uh.

JOAN: Whoever did it slipped a note under the door. It said, "We don't want your kind in our neighborhood."

MIKE: How do you know that?

JOAN: Mr. Zand, my history teacher, told us.

MIKE: The Bowens own that store. What "kind" are they?

JOAN: They're not a *kind*. They're *people*.

MIKE: Yeah. They talk a little differently, but I guess they're OK.

JOAN: There's more. Last week, someone threw eggs at the Handels' house, and two nights ago someone tossed bags of garbage on the Rudlys' lawn.

MIKE: I heard about that. I thought it was just some kids.

JOAN: It's not just kids. It's a hate group.

MIKE: A hate group? That would never happen here.

JOAN: It *is* happening. Mr. Zand got this in the mail. *[She takes a sheet of paper out of her notebook.]* He brought it in to class to show us.

MIKE: *[reading]* "It's time to stop them from taking over our neighborhood. They're animals and savages. We don't want to live near them, and we've had enough. We're going to put a stop to it." *[stops reading]* Mr. Zand got this?

JOAN: Everyone on his block got one.

MIKE: I wonder what the Bowens are going to do.

JOAN: The question is, what are *we* going to do?

MIKE: *We*? What does this have to do with us?

JOAN: The Bowens live in our neighborhood. They're our neighbors.

MIKE: Yeah . . . so?

JOAN: So we're in this, too.

MIKE: What does this have to do with *me*?

JOAN: There's a hate group in your neighborhood.

MIKE: But they're not bothering me.

JOAN: Whose neighborhood *is* this?

MIKE: Mine. Yours.

JOAN: They think it's theirs, and they want to decide who lives here.

MIKE: They won't get away with that.

JOAN: If no one does anything, they might.

MIKE: Oh, no one has to *do* anything. This kind of thing happens once or twice, and everyone gets all excited. Then it just dies down and goes away by itself.

JOAN: What if it doesn't go away? What if it gets worse?

MIKE: OK. Maybe something should be done.

JOAN: Mr. Zand is organizing a rally this afternoon.

MIKE: What good will that do?

JOAN: It will show them they can't do this sort of thing in our neighborhood, and that there are a lot of us who are against them. That way, people who don't agree with them will know they're not alone.

MIKE: Does the hate group know about the rally?

JOAN: I don't know. But they will.

[Hank approaches them, excited.]

HANK: Someone slashed Mr. Zand's tires! The police are on their way.

MIKE: Looks like they know about it, all right.

JOAN: Mr. Zand said this might happen. When you fight back against people like this, they respond with threats. They want to see if you really mean what you say.

MIKE: Maybe they'll be at the rally to see who goes to it.

JOAN: That's the whole point. We *want* them to know so they'll see they don't have any friends in this neighborhood.

MIKE: But what if this stirs them up? Why risk making things worse?

JOAN: They're already getting worse. They've gone from throwing eggs to sending hate mail. Yesterday, they threw paint on the Bowens' store, and now they've slashed Mr. Zand's tires.

MIKE: Well, as long as they don't do anything to *me*.

[Mr. Zand appears.]

HANK: Mr. Zand! How's your car?

MR. ZAND: Two ruined tires. We're moving the rally up to this afternoon. They're saying enough is enough. Well, so are we.

HANK: What time is the rally?

MR. ZAND: I'm on my way over now. Are any of you coming?

HANK: Sure!

JOAN: I am! *[to Mike]* Mike?

MIKE: I don't know.

JOAN: Why not?

MIKE: Well, I was going to study for tomorrow's test.

JOAN: The rally won't take that long. We'll have plenty of time to study.

MIKE: I have some other things to do, too.

MR. ZAND: It's always easy to find a reason to avoid something that's hard.

MIKE: It's not that.

HANK: Do you agree with them?

MIKE: No! I don't agree with them! I think they have to be stopped. But—

MR. ZAND: But why should you be the one to stop them?

MIKE: Yeah.

MR. ZAND: Everyone agrees they should be stopped, but sometimes it's hard to do. So people leave it to someone else. The problem is, if everyone waits for someone else to do something, nothing gets done. Maybe all it takes to stop a thing like this is one person saying it's wrong. That reminds everyone else to stand up and say it, too.

MIKE: But there are plenty of people standing up this time. You don't need me.

MR. ZAND: You can never have too many people involved. The more people they see there, the stronger our message is—it's *our* neighborhood, *they're* the ones who aren't welcome. It also says something about us if we *don't* do anything.

MIKE: That makes sense. But I don't think something like this can be stopped by a rally.

HANK: Then how do you stop it?

MIKE: I don't know. But the rally might make things worse, and *that's* not going to help. Besides, how do you change the way other people feel?

JOAN: So you do nothing?

MIKE: Why do something if it won't help anyway?

MR. ZAND: But maybe this will help.

MIKE: *Maybe.* But why should I put myself on the line for people I don't even know? Especially if no one is bothering *me.*

MR. ZAND: Today it's the Bowens, but how do you know "your kind" won't be next?

MIKE: I'm not a *kind.*

MR. ZAND: Neither are the Bowens.

HANK: Mr. Zand, the rally's going to start.

MR. ZAND: It's up to you, Mike. Your choice.

JOAN: Are you coming with us?

[They all turn to Mike.]

MIKE: Well, . . .

IIIII THINKING ABOUT THE PLAY

1. Is Mike right that this problem will probably go away by itself?
2. Do you agree or disagree with Mike that this isn't his problem because the hate group isn't bothering him? Explain.
3. Why do you think Mike is having trouble believing that the hate group is a real problem?

4. At one point, Mr. Zand says if nothing is done, *that* will say something about the neighborhood. What does he mean by this?

5. Mike gives several reasons why he feels he doesn't have to go the rally. Do you think there might be other reasons that he isn't saying out loud?

IIIII THINKING ABOUT THE ENDING

Mike says he doesn't need to go to the rally because the hate group isn't targeting him, the rally won't help, and he doesn't want to put himself on the line for people he doesn't really know. But his friends think it's important to attend the rally, and Mr. Zand gives several reasons why Mike should be there.

Using what you've learned about the characters, write an ending for the play that takes place after the rally. Include Mike and Joan and any other characters you feel are important to the story. Be sure to include whether or not Mike went to the rally and how he and the others feel about his decision. You might also want to include what happened at the rally.

The Visit

by Brenda Lane Richardson

Characters:
Erica
Erica's mother
Little Sweetness

Scene: *the living room of the apartment Erica shares with her mother. Her mother dusts the tables as Erica sits in a chair pretending to be bored, with her fist supporting her chin.*

MOTHER: Why aren't you helping? She'll be here any minute.

ERICA: You act like some queen is coming. Ma, she's just some girl.

MOTHER: *[pausing in her work]* She's your cousin. You should be proud of her, not jealous. *[looking toward a picture on the wall]* Think how proud your father would be of his sister's little girl. Her winning the Presidential Honors award is such a . . . a . . . *[groping for words]* well, an honor.

ERICA: Big deal. She gets to meet the President.

MOTHER: *[staring dreamily out the window]* . . . *and* have dinner with him and the First Lady. I wonder what they serve at the White House. *[looking back toward Erica]* We're lucky she even wants to stop off here to see us on her way to Washington. *[catching her breath]* She's here. There's her cab now.

ERICA: *[jumping up, pretending to be impressed]* Oh, goody. Why don't you run down, and I'll roll out the red carpet.

[Her mother looks crossly at her and runs out the door.]

ERICA: *[talking to herself]* I don't care what she won. I'll never forgive her for getting me in trouble that time I visited her in Georgia. How was I to know it was a wasps' nest? Little Sweetness told me to throw that rock, and I did. I didn't make the wasps sting Mama. I didn't make Mama's eye swell up from the stings. *[as if she's growing angry all over again, remembering the long-ago trick]* . . . Little Sweetness. I can't believe she's still using that baby name. *[sucking her teeth; then reconsidering the idea]* Well, this *is* the first time I've seen Mama smile since Daddy passed away. *[walking toward the photograph]* I'll try my best to make your niece feel welcome, Daddy. The past is behind us. She has to be nicer than she used to be.

[In the distance, Mother can be heard talking with someone.]

MOTHER: Oh, what pretty shoes, Little Sweetness. And you walk so daintily. Erica's right in here. *[in a voice that sounds more like an order than a conversation]* She's waiting to welcome you, I bet.

[Erica plants a big smile on her face as Little Sweetness is led in. Little Sweetness looks like she has come straight from an old-fashioned movie about the country. She wears a suit, gloves, a hat, and high heels. Smiling warmly, she stiffly embraces Erica and speaks with a heavy Southern accent.]

LITTLE SWEETNESS: Just look at you. You're as perfect as I remembered.

ERICA: *[frowning]* That's what I was thinking about you. *[noticing her mother's scowl, Erica repeats, in a more pleasant voice]* That's just what I was thinking about you. You could have stepped right off the cover of *Seventeen* magazine.

LITTLE SWEETNESS: You like my outfit? I've got lots of them. If we lived closer, I'd let you borrow them. *[Mother steps across the room for a minute, smiling up at the photograph. Little Sweetness whispers.]* But first you'd have to take some weight off those hips of yours. *[When Mother moves in closer again, she abruptly changes the subject and her tone.]* Mama is so excited about the Presidential Honors award. It'll be on CNN. *[looking around the room]* You do have a television, don't you?

ERICA: Yeah, but I've outgrown Mr. Rogers.

LITTLE SWEETNESS: *[whispering, so Erica's mother can't overhear her from where she stands near the photo]* Looks like you're ready for a Halloween special.

[Erica's mother seems unaware of the tension between the two girls. She returns to them smiling, with her arms around them both.]

MOTHER: I'm so glad you two are getting along. Little Sweetness, I fixed you something to eat.

LITTLE SWEETNESS: Aunt Carolyn, you shouldn't have.

MOTHER: Anything for my favorite niece. *[As if suddenly remembering something, she pulls a card from her apron pocket.]* Erica, look what Little Sweetness brought us. A copy of her report card.

LITTLE SWEETNESS: I don't want to brag. My mother insisted I bring it.

MOTHER: *[reading the card]* A's on everything. You won't have trouble getting into college.

LITTLE SWEETNESS: I'm planning to study medicine. So far I've received early admission into Harvard, Howard, Tuskeegee, and Spelman.

MOTHER: Just think, a doctor in the family.

ERICA: *[Behind her mother's back, Erica sticks a finger down her throat and mutters.]* I could use one now.

MOTHER: I've got to run to the store before I put dinner on the table.

LITTLE SWEETNESS: Oh, please, can't I help?

MOTHER: You're company. You and Erica should spend time getting to know each other.

ERICA: What time did you say you were leaving?

MOTHER: *[outraged]* Erica!

ERICA: I want to make sure we make every moment count.

[Smiling uncertainly, her mother leaves. Little Sweetness plops into a chair, tosses her hat across the room, pulls out a cigarette, and lights up. Erica is astonished.]

ERICA: Are you crazy? Do you realize that cigarettes killed 45,000 black people last year? *[Little Sweetness ignores her. Erica moves to the photo on the wall, her voice cracking]* Including my daddy.

LITTLE SWEETNESS: Well, I'm not your daddy, so get off my back.

ERICA: *[walking with determination toward Little Sweetness]* I will not let you use that poison in my house. *[She snatches the cigarette from her cousin. Just then, the door swings open. It's Mother.]*

MOTHER: I'm so excited, I forgot my purse. *[She is stunned into silence as she sees Erica holding a cigarette.]* Erica, how could you? And after all we went through with your daddy.

ERICA: Mom—

1. Why do you think Erica was so annoyed about her cousin's visit?

2. Was Erica's mother being fair to Erica? Why?

3. How do you think it made Erica feel to hear her mother continue to praise Little Sweetness? Explain.

4. Why do you think Little Sweetness behaved as she did?

5. How would you compare Erica and Little Sweetness?

IIII■ THINKING ABOUT THE ENDING

Think about what you learned about the characters. Will Erica tell her mother the truth? If she does, how will she convince her mother that it is the truth?

Write an ending for the play based on what you know about Erica. Use what you have learned about the characters to write Little Sweetness's lines. Include Erica's mother's response as well.

Dim Sum for Two

by Kipp Erante Cheng

Characters:
Lisa
Tom
John
Rich

Scene One: *a Chinese restaurant in New York City. Lisa and Tom sit on chairs, but face and address the audience.*

LISA: My name is Lisa.

TOM: And I'm Tom.

LISA: This is our first date.

TOM: The first of many to come, I hope.

LISA: I hope we get along.

TOM: I hope this date goes well.

LISA: Do you think I look all right?

TOM: Maybe I shouldn't have worn so much cologne.

LISA: The first time I saw Tom was in chemistry class. He was wearing this beautiful blue sweater, and he kept staring at me.

TOM: I hope Lisa didn't think I was being too obvious the first time I saw her. I didn't wear my glasses that day, and I kept squinting just to get a clear look at her. I thought she was beautiful.

LISA: When Tom asked me out last Thursday, right after class, I was surprised and happy that he'd noticed me.

TOM: I was surprised that Lisa agreed to go out with me. She's popular at school, smart and funny. What else could a guy ask for?

Scene Two: *a table in the restaurant. Tom and Lisa are facing each other.*

LISA: I like this restaurant.

TOM: Me too. Have you been here before?

LISA: No. I don't really like Chinese food.

TOM: Really? I thought that because—

LISA: What? Because I was Chinese American I would like Chinese food?

TOM: Well, yeah. I guess. You don't like Chinese food?

LISA: No, I'd rather have pizza. But this is fine. For our first date.

TOM: Good. I'm glad. So have you ever been to China?

LISA: No. I was born in America. Have you ever been to Ireland?

TOM: What?

LISA: You're Irish, right?

TOM: But I was born in America.

LISA: Me too. So why would you assume that I had ever been to China?

TOM: You're right. I wasn't thinking. I'm sorry.

LISA: Tom, we're more alike than you might think.

TOM: Yeah, I guess you're right.

LISA: I mean, just because we don't have the same background doesn't mean that we're all that different. Both of our families came to America for similar reasons.

TOM: Right. To find a better life. To come to the new country.

LISA: Do you think it would bother your friends that I'm not blonde and blue-eyed?

TOM: Not at all. I don't think my friends are like that. Would your friends be bothered?

LISA: No, I don't think so.

TOM: I mean, I know some jerks at school who call Chinese Americans by some nasty names. But I'm not like that at all. Really, I think people are all pretty much the same.

LISA: That's great, Tom. *[She smiles at him as Tom's friends John and Rich enter.]*

JOHN: Hey, Tom! Is this Lisa?

RICH: Yeah! She looks great!

TOM: Yes, this is Lisa. Lisa, this is John and Rich.

LISA: Hi.

RICH: Tom, you didn't tell us how pretty Lisa is. You said she was just another Chinese girl.

TOM: Rich, shut up.

LISA: Did you say that, Tom?

TOM: No, I didn't. These guys are jerks. They must have misunderstood me.

JOHN: What are you talking about, Tom? You said that Lisa was another Lotus Blossom—

LISA: What? I can't believe this! I thought you were different, Tom.

TOM: *[to Rich and John]* Would you just *shut up*? *[Turning to Lisa, Tom is uncomfortable]* I *am* different from these guys. I don't know what they're talking about. I mean, maybe I said some mean things about you, but that was before I met you. Now that I sort of know you, I know you're not like all the other girls at school—

LISA: And what is that supposed to mean?

JOHN: *[angry at Tom's remarks about him]* Yeah, Tom. What are you talking about?

RICH: He's singing a different tune now, Lisa. Mr Tolerance here said some pretty interesting things about Asians. Do you want to hear them, Lisa?

LISA: You're a jerk!

TOM: *[through clenched teeth to Rich and John]* Get out of here! *[to Lisa]* Lisa! You have to believe me! These things that John and Rich are saying are lies! I don't think those things about you!

LISA: How can I believe a word you say to me?

RICH: You shouldn't, Lisa. Hey, if you're finished with Tom, maybe you'd like to go out with me some time?

LISA: You've got to be kidding.

JOHN: Hey Lisa, maybe you have a sister you can set me up with.

LISA: Right.

TOM: Will you leave her *alone*! You guys don't know the first thing about her.

JOHN: Oh yeah? And you do? All I know is that you're trashing us now the way you trashed her before.

TOM: Get *out* of here!

JOHN: Fine. We know the two of you want to be alone.

RICH: Have fun, Tom. And Lisa, if you want my number, it's in the book.

LISA: *[disgusted]* Jerks!

TOM: I'm sorry, Lisa. I can't believe this. It's all just a huge misunderstanding. Those guys don't know what they're talking about. I really like you. I hope you believe me. Don't take their word over mine.

LISA: How can I believe you? I mean, I trusted you, and then your so-called friends come and say all of these horrible things about me and tell me all of these horrible things you've said about me. What should I believe?

TOM: Look, I admit that before I met you, I made a lot of assumptions about you. Maybe I didn't have a very clear idea about the kind of person you really are. But now that I got a chance to talk to you and really get to know you, I feel totally different. I want us to be friends. I want us to go out again. I really like you, Lisa.

LISA: Tom, before I met you I had some ideas about you, too. But I didn't talk to my friends about you and ruin your reputation just because I didn't understand. I tried to give you the benefit of the doubt, and now I don't know what I'm supposed to think about you. I thought you were different. I thought I could really trust you—

TOM: *[pleading]* You can trust me, Lisa. Really. I really like you. Don't let John and Rich spoil your ideas about me. What do you want to do, Lisa? I'm so sorry about this. I'll take you home. Do you want to go home?

LISA: Tom, you tell me. How would you feel if you were in my shoes?

TOM: I guess I would feel pretty bad.

LISA: Right, you would.

TOM: So what do you want to do?

LISA: Oh, I don't know, Tom. I don't know.

TOM: Well, whatever you decide, I'll understand.

LISA: . . .

IIIII THINKING ABOUT THE PLAY

1. What kinds of expectations do Tom and Lisa have for their first date?

2. What assumptions do Tom and Lisa make about each other based on their heritage?

3. Why do you think John and Rich treat Lisa the way they do?

4. Do you think that Tom has really changed the way he feels?

5. What do you think Tom should have said to his friends? How else could he have handled the situation?

Tom and Lisa's first date starts to go wrong when Tom's friends from school barge in on their conversation. Lisa must choose between believing Tom and believing his friends. Whom should she trust in this situation? What might you do?

Write an ending in which Lisa makes a decision. Does she stay, or does she walk out on Tom? Include Tom's reaction to Lisa's decision.

Kid Brother

by Cary Pepper

Characters:
Linda
Mother
Tony

Scene: the living room of a city apartment. Linda sprawls on the couch, talking on the phone. Her mother moves around the apartment, setting things in order and picking up baby toys from the floor.

LINDA: You're kidding! Are you sure she's coming? I thought she and Theresa weren't talking to each other. . . . They had this huge argument. . . . Over Bobby, that's what! I thought they'd never be in the same room again. . . . *Who's* coming? I didn't know Theresa knew him! . . . I don't, but I'd sure like to!

MOTHER: Who's on the phone?

LINDA: Hold on. *[to mother]* Vanessa.

MOTHER: *[smiles and rolls her eyes]* You're gonna see her in half an hour.

LINDA: We're bringing each other up to date.

MOTHER: Well, how about getting off and helping me bring this house up to date?

LINDA: Yeah, OK. *[speaking into the phone]* Gotta go. See you later. Don't forget to bring that new CD! *[She hangs up.]* What do you want me to do?

MOTHER: Could you please take out the trash?

LINDA: Mom, it's Saturday night.

MOTHER: Does the trash know that? I just want you to throw it away, not date it.

LINDA: You work too hard.

MOTHER: Now that's the truth.

LINDA: You should learn to relax.

MOTHER: I don't have to *learn* to relax. I need the *time* to relax.

LINDA: What are you doing tonight?

MOTHER: There's a great movie on TV. I'm going to make a huge bowl of popcorn, sit on the couch, put my feet up, and . . . relax.

LINDA: You ought to have fun.

MOTHER: You're right. Maybe I'll come to your party.

LINDA: I don't think you'd find it that much fun.

MOTHER: Relax, Lin . . . Just kidding. After the week I put in, I can't think of anything I'd rather do more than absolutely nothing.

[Linda goes into the kitchen, comes out with a large, full trash bag, and leaves. Her mother picks up a toy and starts toward the bedroom. The phone rings.]

MOTHER: Which one of them is it now? *[answering the phone]* Hello? . . . Oh, hi, Katherine. I thought it was one of Linda's friends. They're having a party tonight, and she's been on the phone with almost every one of them. . . . I know we used to do that too. It's just weird seeing *her* do it. . . . Me? Nothing. . . . Oh, I'm sorry to hear that. . . . Tonight? I guess so. I'll have to rearrange some things. Linda will have to take care of Henry. . . . No, I'm just thinking out loud. I owe you this, and it's time-and-a-half. I can't afford to turn it down. Eight to midnight. Okay. And don't worry. I'm sure your mother will be all right. . . . Bye.

[She hangs up. Linda returns.]

LINDA: Anything else?

MOTHER: Oh, yeah. And you're not going to like it.

LINDA: I'm not doing the laundry!

MOTHER: When you hear this, you'll wish it *was* laundry. Katherine just called. She was supposed to work tonight, but her mother is sick, and she has to go over there. She asked if I could do the first part of her shift, and I told her I would. So . . .

LINDA: No.

MOTHER: No, what?

LINDA: You want me to baby-sit Henry.

MOTHER: Do I have any other choice?

LINDA: Do *I* have a choice?

MOTHER: I know you had plans for tonight, but this—

LINDA: I *have* plans. I *had* plans and I still *have* them.

MOTHER: Linda . . .

LINDA: You said it was all right.

MOTHER: I know that. But I owe Katherine this. She did it for me last month when Henry was sick. And we can use the money. It's time-and-a-half.

LINDA: It's Saturday night!

MOTHER: That's why it's time-and-a-half.

LINDA: But it's Saturday night!

MOTHER: Linda, people work on Saturday night. You think I want to do this? I don't. But a friend needs a favor. And it benefits you, too. What do you think I'm going to spend the money on? You, me, and Henry.

LINDA: You said I could do this.

MOTHER: Yes, I did. But sometimes things change. We don't always get what we want. It's only half a shift.

LINDA: So what?

MOTHER: I don't know. Look, I'm sorry this happened. But you see these kids all the time. You can hang out with them some other night.

LINDA: You don't understand. You pretend you do, but you don't.

MOTHER: I do understand. Believe it or not, I was your age too, once. This just has to be done. End of discussion. I have to get dressed.

LINDA: Can they come over here?

MOTHER: No. The last time you did that when you were watching Henry, you forgot all about him.

LINDA: He's 3 years old! All he does is sleep!

MOTHER: Then how come he got out of bed and broke the lamp?

LINDA: Mom . . .

MOTHER: End of discussion.

[Mother goes into the bedroom. Linda throws herself down on the couch and broods. A few minutes later, Mother emerges from the bedroom wearing a nurse's uniform.]

MOTHER: I'll be back as early as I can. If it's not too late, maybe you can still go to the party. It's just down the hall.

[Linda doesn't respond.]

MOTHER: Linda?

LINDA: This isn't fair.

MOTHER: I know. I'll make it up to you.

LINDA: Oh yeah? How?

MOTHER: I don't know. I'll try to think of something. *[Linda doesn't respond.]* Linda . . . ?

LINDA: What?

MOTHER: You know how much I depend on you. To help out around the house and do what needs doing.

LINDA: *[pouting]* Uh-huh.

MOTHER: OK. See you later, Lin.

[She waits for a few seconds, but Linda doesn't respond. She leaves. Linda continues to brood; then she gets up, goes to the bedroom, and peers in.]

LINDA: Little brat. All you're gonna do is sleep all night.

[She goes back to the couch and throws herself down. After a few minutes, the doorbell rings. Linda goes to the door and opens it. Tony walks in.]

TONY: Ready?

LINDA: I was. My mom has to work. I have to stay here with Henry.

TONY: You said she was off tonight.

LINDA: She was. She's doing someone else's shift.

TONY: You're gonna miss a great party.

LINDA: Thanks a lot, Tony! *That* makes me feel better! I was thinking. . . . Maybe everyone could come over here.

TONY: No way. I just found out Theresa's parents are away for the whole night. And your mom won't be.

LINDA: Well, they could come here, and we could move over there when she comes home.

TONY: They'll never go for it.

LINDA: Yeah. That *is* a stupid idea. If my mom found out, she'd kill me.

TONY: I've got a better idea. Come to Theresa's and bring Henry with you.

LINDA: You think so?

TONY: All he does is sleep. He can do that there as well as here.

LINDA: But if my mom finds out . . .

TONY: How's she gonna know?

LINDA: If he wakes up, he'll tell her.

TONY: OK, I got a *better* idea. Come to the party and leave early. You can be back before your mom gets home. She'll never know.

LINDA: What about Henry?

TONY: Leave him here.

LINDA: I can't do that.

TONY: Why not? All he does is sleep. He'll never know, so he won't be able to tell.

LINDA: What if he wakes up?

TONY: OK, you can come back here to check on him. Say, every half hour. It's just down the hall.

LINDA: What if my mom gets home early?

TONY: You'll be able to see her coming from Theresa's window. You'll have plenty of time to get back before she does. She'll never know you were gone.

LINDA: What if my mom comes home, and I don't see her?

TONY: We'll help you watch for her. We'll take turns checking the window.

LINDA: If my mom finds out, she'll be *really* angry.

TONY: Hey, what if you were here, watching the brat, and you needed to borrow, I don't know, some milk or something. You'd go over to Theresa's, borrow the milk, and come back. Right?

LINDA: I guess.

TONY: Well, this is the same thing.

LINDA: You think I can pull it off?

TONY: Absolutely! What are you going to do if you stay here? Watch him sleep?

LINDA: *[thinking]* I still don't know.

TONY: Well, you can do whatever you want to. But there's no way *I'd* miss this party. *[He goes to the door.]* Are you coming or not?

[Linda looks toward the bedroom and then looks at Tony.]

LINDA: . . .

IIIII THINKING ABOUT THE PLAY

1. Describe the relationship between Linda and her mother.
2. What kind of person do you think Linda is? Why do you think this?
3. Is Linda's mother right to make Linda cancel her plans so that she can watch Henry? Why or why not?
4. Is Linda right to be angry about having to stay home? Why or why not?
5. What do you think of Tony's idea, which would allow Linda to go to the party?

Linda really wants to go to this party, but at the last minute her mother tells her to stay home and baby-sit her younger brother. Tony thinks he has found a way she can do both. Linda has to decide whether she'll obey her mother or do what *she* wants. Think about what you learned about Linda. Do you think she'll go to the party or stay home? Is there a way to deal with this problem that Linda hasn't thought of?

Write an ending for the play that includes what Linda decides, as well as a scene between Linda and her mother when her mother returns home.

On the D Train

by Cecilia Rubino

Characters:
Joey
Steven
Mike
Jennifer

Scene: *on a subway platform. A train screeches into the station, and Joey steps into the first car. He checks the crowded train and then quickly steps back out. As the train pulls out of the station, Joey sits back down and opens a huge textbook. Mike and Steven rush onto the platform, carrying backpacks.*

STEVEN: It's gone! Man, this happens every morning.

MIKE: It's only 10 after. We'll make it.

STEVEN: Hey, Joey! Joey, how's it going, man?

MIKE: Hey, Joey, where've you been all week?

JOEY: *[closing his book]* What's up, guys?

MIKE: Hey, Joey, what's with the glasses, man? You don't wear glasses. *[Mike reaches to grab the glasses off Joey's nose.]*

JOEY: Come on, Mikey. Don't break those. I need them when I read.

MIKE: Yeah, right.

STEVEN: Naaaah. It's not just the glasses. What's wrong with you, Joey? You look different. You look good. He looks nice, doesn't he, Mikey?

JOEY: I just got my hair cut.

MIKE: It looks good. Nice. But what did you do to your face? You shave? *[Mike taps Joey's cheek.]*

JOEY: Hey, keep your hands off my face and give me the glasses back.

STEVEN: What's this, Einstein? A little light reading? *[Steven grabs the book from under Joey's arm and tosses it to Mike.]*

MIKE: *[paging through the book]* Calculus! Since when do you take calculus?

STEVEN: He's in calculus, and *I'm* Einstein.

JOEY: Come on, you guys.

STEVEN: Joey, what's going on, you showing us up? Mikey, come here, smell this. *[Steven and Mike lean toward Joey and take a deep breath in unison.]* What is that? After-shave?

MIKE: You smell like my girl.

JOEY: *[grabbing back his book and glasses]* Get off my case, you guys.

MIKE: If I didn't know you better, I'd say you were selling out on us.

STEVEN: That's not it. Put it on the table, Joey. Who is she? Who're you trying to impress?

MIKE: You got a girl, Joey? Since when did you get a girl?

STEVEN: Does she go to Lincoln?

MIKE: She's a freshman, right?

JOEY: No, no. All right, I'll tell you. I'm trying to get with this girl.

MIKE: Anybody we know?

JOEY: No. Her name's Jennifer.

MIKE: Not Jennifer Ramirez?

JOEY: No. You don't know her. I don't really know her. She goes to Murrow. I keep seeing her on the train, right around 7:20, 7:30. Sits in the first car every morning. She's incredible. I can't stop thinking about her.

STEVEN: A girl from Murrow?

MIKE: Those girls are too smart. They're stuck up.

STEVEN: Joey, have you even talked to this girl?

JOEY: No. That's the problem. She never looks up. She's always studying some calculus book. So I figured if I got a book like hers, then maybe she'd see me, and we'd have something to talk about.

MIKE: Joey, don't think so much. All you gotta do is walk up to her and start talking.

JOEY: I can't. I just can't do it. I don't want her to think I'm an idiot, just trying to hit on her like a million other guys. I don't want to blow it. This girl is special.

MIKE: But Joey, you don't even know her.

JOEY: I'm serious.

STEVEN: Joey, you ask me, you're going about this all wrong. What happens if she starts talking to you and finds out you don't know calculus from a hole in the wall? Don't be so down on yourself! So maybe she's smart. No girl wants to go out with a geek. You just got to get her to notice you . . .

MIKE: Break the ice. Pick up a pen; ask her if she dropped it.

STEVEN: Girls like a guy who's smooth, you know . . .

MIKE: Confident.

STEVEN: But not a jerk.

MIKE: Definitely not a jerk. Steve, tell him about how you met Melissa.

STEVEN: You mean when I threw gum in her hair?

JOEY: You threw gum in her hair?

MIKE: A wad, like this big!

STEVEN: Yeah, you know, it was an accident. Mikey popped his head into my social studies class. I was trying to finish a quiz, and here he was bothering me. So I took the gum out of my mouth to throw it at him. Just then Melissa stood up, and the gum got stuck right in her hair.

JOEY: I'm not throwing gum in anyone's hair.

STEVEN: You just don't get it. Man! If you really want to get with this girl, you can't sit back and hope she'll notice you. You've got to make something happen.

JOEY: Like what?

STEVEN: OK, stand back, I have an idea. Joey, don't say we never did anything for you. You got to pretend you don't know us, OK? I'm gonna get on the train and act like some kind of bum.

MIKE: That should be easy for you.

STEVEN: Make yourself useful, Mikey. Give me your jacket. This is a bum's jacket.

MIKE: Thank you. Pull your hat down. Yeah, untie your shoes, and let me have your pack.

STEVEN: So Joey, here's the plan. I bump into this girl, give her a hard time. Make like I'm going to rip her off or something. You jump in there and help her out. Got it?

MIKE: Here comes the train.

STEVEN: She'll be eating out of your hand in no time.

JOEY: *[looking uncertain]* What am I supposed to do?

STEVEN: You figure it out. Just remember, you've never seen us before.

[The train pulls into the station, and the boys step into the first car.]

MIKE: Is she here?

JOEY: That's her. The one with the book.

[Jennifer is holding onto the center pole of the subway car, balancing a huge math book in one hand.]

MIKE: Now that is a beautiful girl.

STEVEN: Back me up, Mikey. *[Steven makes his way through the car and bumps into Jennifer.]* This is a public train, Miss, can we get through?

JENNIFER: Excuse me?

STEVEN: What's your problem, girl? You got a problem with me? *[Jennifer avoids his eyes and turns away.]* What, you won't look at me? What, I'm not a person to you?

JENNIFER: What is your problem?

STEVEN: What, you can't even look at me? You can't apologize? *[He pushes her book.]* Ooooooh, calculus, you think you're too good for me!

JOEY: Hey, stop bothering her, man.

STEVEN: What's it to you?

JOEY: Just stop bothering her.

STEVEN: She should try being more polite next time!

[Steven reaches out and grabs the chain from around Jennifer's neck.]

JENNIFER: Oh my God, he's got my chain! He's got my chain!

JOEY: *[grabs Steven from behind and wrenches his arm behind his back]* Don't think you're going anywhere with that. Drop it, man. I said drop it! *[Steven drops the chain and runs out of the car with Mike as the doors open at the next station.]*

JOEY: This is your stop, right?

JENNIFER: Yeah, how did you know? They didn't hurt you, did they?

JOEY: Nah, they're just jerks. Here, you'll have to get this fixed. *[Joey hands the chain back to Jennifer as they get off the train.]*

JENNIFER: Thank you so much. Most people wouldn't have done that, you know. I mean, did you see everybody else just sitting there?

JOEY: You go to Murrow, right?

JENNIFER: Yeah. Those guys really shook me up.

JOEY: I've seen you on this train before.

JENNIFER: Yeah? You were so great. What did you say your name was?

JOEY: Joey.

JENNIFER: Joey. Hi, I'm Jennifer.

JOEY: I have to wait for the next train. I have a couple more stops to go.

JENNIFER: Oh no, I'm making you late!

JOEY: Don't worry about it.

JENNIFER: Listen, I really don't think I can go to first period. I need to get my head together. Maybe we can get a cup of coffee or something.

JOEY: Sure.

JENNIFER: There's this place right upstairs. *[pointing at the platform]* Joey, look. The cops have those two guys, the guys from the train. I'm sure it's them. See that other guy with the cops? He was on the train with us. He must have seen the whole thing and got that cop to come over. We need to go over there and—

JOEY: *[hesitating]* Jennifer, I . . .

|||||| THINKING ABOUT THE PLAY

1. Why is Joey shy about meeting Jennifer?

2. Steven and Mike think Joey looks different. What has changed about him?

3. Why do you think Joey's friends tease him about his new look?

4. What does Steven mean when he tells Joey that he can't just sit back, that he's got to "make something happen"? Do you agree with this?

5. How would you describe Joey? How would you describe Mike and Steven?

|||■THINKING ABOUT THE ENDING

Think about what you have learned about Joey, Steven, Mike, and Jennifer. What do you think Joey will say to Jennifer? Joey risks losing the girl of his dreams if he confesses the scam and helps out his friends. How do you think Jennifer would react if she found out the truth?

Write an ending for the play in which you use what you have learned about the characters to predict how Joey will react. Include the reactions of the other characters as well as Joey's response.

Setting an Example

by Steven Otfinoski

Characters:
Hector
Man 1
Man 2
Juan

Scene: *a downtown street in front of a liquor store, 15 minutes before the store closes. Hector, 15, is standing in front of the liquor store. He clutches a five-dollar bill in his hand. A man in his 30s heads for the liquor store. Hector stops him.*

HECTOR: Hey, mister—

MAN 1: Yes?

HECTOR: Could you do me a favor?

MAN 1: What kind of favor?

HECTOR: Could you buy me a pint of gin while you're in the liquor store?

MAN 1: *[staring at Hector]* Why can't you go in and buy it yourself?

HECTOR: I would, but the guy in there won't sell to me.

MAN 1: You mean he won't because you're underage and it's against the law.

HECTOR: That's right. That's why I need your help. I got five dollars here for the pint. You can keep the change.

MAN 1: That's very generous, but I'm I can't help you, kid.

HECTOR: Why not?

MAN 1: What if someone found out that I bought liquor for an underage kid? I don't need that kind of trouble.

HECTOR: Aw, come on, mister. No one's going to know!

MAN 1: I'm sorry.

[The man turns away and walks into the liquor store. Another man, in his late 20s, steps forward. He has been listening to Hector and the first man.]

MAN 2: Got a problem, eh, kid?

HECTOR: Yeah, I'll say!

MAN 2: That guy was a jerk. I know how you feel.

HECTOR: You do?

MAN 2: Sure. I was your age once. I know what it's like not to be able to get any booze when everyone else is drinking and having a good time.

HECTOR: It's tough.

MAN 2: Don't worry. I'll get your gin for you.

HECTOR: You will?

MAN 2: Sure. I like to help people. Especially a nice young guy like you.

HECTOR: Thanks, mister. You're a real pal.

MAN 2: Don't mention it. Just give me that five, and I'll be back in a flash.

[Hector hands the man his five dollars.]

MAN 2: You just wait right here.

[Hector watches the man go into the store. Juan, a 10 year old, comes up to Hector.]

JUAN: Hey, mister—

HECTOR: [turning in surprise] Are you talking to me?

JUAN: Yeah. Could you help me out?

HECTOR: What do you want?

JUAN: I need a pint of gin. Could you buy it for me?

HECTOR: I can't— *[Hector stops as he looks closely at Juan.]* How old are you?

JUAN: Old enough.

HECTOR: Don't get wise. I asked you how old you are.

JUAN: I'm 10. Well, almost 11.

HECTOR: A kid your age shouldn't be drinking. You're too young.

JUAN: That's my business.

HECTOR: I got a brother your age. If I ever caught him drinking, I'd—

JUAN: I don't want to hear about your brother. I just want a pint of gin. Here's my five dollars. You can keep the change.

HECTOR: No way, man.

JUAN: Come on! That liquor store's going to close in five minutes! Help me out!

HECTOR: You don't belong on the street this late. You should be home in bed.

JUAN: Who do you think you are? My father or something?

HECTOR: Go on! Get out of here! Beat it!

JUAN: You can't tell me to beat it. It's a free country!

HECTOR: Listen, kids your age shouldn't be drinking. It's wrong.

JUAN: Why?

HECTOR: You can destroy your body. Haven't they told you that at school?

JUAN: Yeah, sure. It's a lot of garbage.

HECTOR: You could damage your brain, your whole body.

JUAN: I don't suppose you ever drink, huh?

HECTOR: [hestitating] No, I don't. And you shouldn't either. Now beat it!

[As they argue, Man 2 comes out of the store. He holds two paper bags in his arms.]

MAN 2: I got your pint, kid. *[seeing Juan]* Who's this?

JUAN: *[staring at Hector]*: This guy bought *you* booze?

HECTOR: I told you to beat it, didn't I?

JUAN: So booze is bad for you, huh? Some joke you are! You're just like my old man—saying one thing and doing another!

MAN 2: What's this punk talking about?

JUAN: I'm no punk! Hey, if you can buy a pint for him, how about one for me, too?

MAN 2: *[to Hector]* Is he a friend of yours?

HECTOR: No!

MAN 2: Well, here's your gin. Enjoy.

[He holds out the bag with the pint of gin to Hector. Hector looks at it for a long moment. Juan watches him.]

MAN 2: What are you waiting for? You want it, don't you?

HECTOR: I . . .

IIIII THINKING ABOUT THE PLAY

1. Why does the first man refuse to buy the gin for Hector?

2. Why do you think the second man does buy the gin for Hector?

3. Why was Hector angry when Juan was only doing the same thing Hector was doing himself?

4. Why do you think Hector lied to Juan about his drinking?

5. Would you feel responsible if a younger brother or sister developed a bad habit by imitating what you did? Explain your answer.

Think about what has happened in the play up to this point. Do you think Hector will take the pint of gin? Why or why not? Do you think his encounter with Juan will have any impact on his actions?

Write an ending for the play in which you use what you have learned about the characters to predict whether or not Hector will take the gin. In your ending, have Hector explain his decision. Include the other characters' reactions as well.

Voices From the Mirror

by Joyce Haines

Characters:
Rose
Rose's reflection in the mirror
Grandmother's image in the mirror
Stage Manager
Heather
Jimmy Bearclaw

Scene One: *a small dressing room in a Broadway theater in New York City. Rose is sitting at her table, staring at her reflection in the mirror, with a make-up brush in her hand. She is wearing a skimpy buckskin costume. On the table are three smudged envelopes (postmarked New Mexico), a small pottery bowl decorated with a Zuni symbol of a rainbird, a Native American headdress with neon-colored feathers, and a playbill announcing* Annie Oakley Rides Again. *A calendar on the wall, with a picture of a desert landscape, is turned to April.*

ROSE: *[speaking to her reflection]* Well, Rose, you're here at last! You're becoming a star.

HER REFLECTION: How does it feel to be a lead dancer rather than a visitor? If only your Zuni cousins could see you now! After seven years, you're finally here.

ROSE: I knew that some good would come out of that dance

tour. Imagine! Me in Chicago playing a pioneer woman in *Appalachian Spring.*

HER REFLECTION: When the time came, when Helen came down with the flu, you were ready. Your movements were perfect. You didn't miss a beat. You mastered every expression, every gesture.

ROSE: And now, this musical. The producers promised an almost guaranteed run of a year.

HER REFLECTION: But this show is going to be totally different from anything you've ever done. It might not be what you expect.

ROSE: Well, it's certainly not what I had in mind when I won that minority dance scholarship.

HER REFLECTION: You signed the contract for this new show pretty fast. Did you even bother to read the script?

ROSE: Who cares what it says? I'll make more money in this show than anyone else back on the reservation could ever hope to earn. Even the best pottery makers would have to work for at least three months to earn what I will make just this first month. Now I can really help out my family, buy them some of the things they've never had. I can even start saving for grandfather's eye operation.

HER REFLECTION: You're glad that you turned down that offer from the American Indian Dance theater last year?

ROSE: Right. I refuse to limit myself to one type of dance. And I won't be tied to only Native American themes, even if . . .

HER REFLECTION: You're getting homesick from reading those letters again, aren't you? Or are you still angry because the producers insisted on billing you as an Apache?

ROSE: Can you believe it? They told me that ticket buyers never heard of Zunis.

GRANDMOTHER'S IMAGE: *[She wears a traditional Zuni dress and holds a small Zuni bowl with a rainbird design.]* Walk tall, my child. But listen to your inner voice before you bend to the words of others. Always remember where you came from. You are a daughter of *A-pi-thlan-shi-wa-ni*, the Priests of the Bow, and the *Akâkâkwe*, the Dance People. Our clan has been in charge of rituals from the beginning of time. Always protect the rituals just as you protect this olla that I made for you, just as I protect the olla that my grandmother made for me when I entered the world.

ROSE: *[respectfully, as she glances at the small bowl sitting in front of the mirror]* *É-lah-kwa.* Thank you, Grandmother, I will never forget your words.

STAGE MANAGER: [*shouting and angry, as he puts his head in the doorway*] Sarah Dancing Bear! Sarah Dancing Bear! Third call, Rose!

Scene Two: *a large stage decorated in Western style. Heather stands in front of a large tepee. Rose runs onto the stage, where she takes her place between the tepee and Annie Oakley's wagon. As she moves, Rose attempts to cover her thighs, which are exposed by high slits in her dress.*

ROSE: I'm sorry. I didn't hear you.

STAGE MANAGER: [*sarcastically*] Yes, yes, Dancing Bear. You're always sorry about something. But if you want to continue being Annie's faithful Indian guide, you'd better start paying attention. You forgot your headdress again. And what happened to the twinkle lights on your bodice?

ROSE: [*adjusting a small battery sewn inside the front of her buckskin dress*] I'm sorry . . .

HEATHER: [*whispering*] Don't let him get your goat. He knows how much this part means to you. At least your body's covered. The rest of us "Indian maidens" are practically naked.

JIMMY BEARCLAW: [*running toward Rose, carrying her headdress*] Here it is, Rose.

ROSE: *É-lah-kwa.*

JIMMY BEARCLAW: *Ho.*

STAGE MANAGER: [*mumbling under his breath*] These people *still* can't speak English.

Scene Three: *Rose's dressing room. The calendar is turned to May. On her dressing table are several pages of blank paper, an envelope, and a pen.*

ROSE: [speaking to the reflection in her dressing room mirror] Now I'm glad I didn't buy those airplane tickets. Opening night would be too much for my family, especially Grandmother.

HER REFLECTION: And what about all the nights after that? What are you going to do about those nights?

ROSE: I can't ever let them see this terrible show. Those stupid producers think all native people look alike, talk alike, wear the same clothes, live in the same kinds of houses, and eat the same food. To them, the Marau, the dance of the Hopi Women's Society, is exactly the same as our Zuni *Thla'-he-kwe* [corn dance]. Jimmy Bearclaw is the only other real native in this whole production. [She picks up her grandmother's olla, holds it in her hands, and then gently puts it down as tears fill her eyes.] If I quit the show now, I'll probably never dance on Broadway again. But I can't stand this any longer.

HER REFLECTION: But what about helping your family? What about the money? It's come in pretty handy since your father lost his job. And what about your grandfather's eye operation? This isn't just you, Rose. Other people are counting on you.

ROSE: [shouting at her reflection] No! Stop it! You've got to stop it!

HEATHER: [knocking on the dressing room door] Are you OK in there? We have to be on stage in 10 minutes.

ROSE: Yes, thanks, it's nothing. I'm just practicing my lines. I'll be right out.

STAGE MANAGER: [poking his head in the door without knocking. He enters and carelessly smashes his cigar butt in Rose's olla.] Hey, babe, let's get a move on. You've got to hustle if you want your name in lights. This is your last chance.

Rose: [*She stares at her reflection in the mirror, reaches tentatively for the jar of makeup remover, and then puts her face in her hands and cries.*] Grandmother, please tell me what to do now. [*Rose looks up into the mirror once again.*]

Her Reflection: Well, Rose, what's it going to be?

Rose: . . .

|||||THINKING ABOUT THE PLAY

1. What did Rose hope for when she left home?
2. What does Rose's grandmother mean when she tells Rose to remember where she came from?
3. Why is the olla important to Rose?
4. Why do you think Rose talks to herself in the mirror instead of confiding in Heather or Jimmy?
5. Why do you think Rose becomes more and more disturbed about the play during the weeks of practice?

|||||THINKING ABOUT THE ENDING

What do you think are the advantages and disadvantages of Rose's leading role in the show? Do you think she will quit? Why or why not? Is there another way she can resolve her problem?

Write an ending to the play that describes Rose's thoughts and actions as she makes her decision and answers the reflection in the mirror.

Someone to Believe In

by Cary Pepper

Characters:
Susan
Pat
Father

Scene: *Susan's bedroom. Susan is at her desk, filling out papers.*

FATHER: *[offstage]* Pat!

[At the sound of her father's voice, Susan looks up and frowns. Then she hides the papers beneath some others on her desk.]

PAT: *[offstage]* What?

FATHER: "What?"! I'm calling you. Are you too lazy to come into the living room?

[Susan makes a face toward the other room.]

PAT: Okay . . . I'm coming.

[the sound of Pat walking into another room]

PAT: What is it, Daddy?

FATHER: You're just like your sister! You two are the laziest people in the world!

[Susan frowns again and then takes out the papers, studies them, and begins to write. After a few minutes, the door opens. Susan quickly hides the papers. Pat is standing in the doorway.]

SUSAN: *[relieved]* Oh, it's you.

PAT: You busy?

SUSAN: Kind of . . . but come in.

[Pat comes in, closing the door behind her.]

SUSAN: What'd he want this time?

PAT: Who knows? He was so busy telling me how lazy we are that he forgot to tell me why he called me.

SUSAN: *[imitating Father]* "You two are the laziest people in the world!"

PAT: *[laughing]* That's it! You do it better than he does!

SUSAN: No one does it better than he does.

PAT: What are you doing?

SUSAN: What do you mean?

PAT: You said you were busy. What are you doing?

[Susan glances at the door; then she eases the hidden papers out from under the others.]

PAT: You decided to go for it?

SUSAN: I think so.

PAT: All right, Suz! Does he know?

SUSAN: Are you crazy? You think *I'm* crazy?

PAT: What if he finds out?

SUSAN: Oh, I'll tell him. . . . But only if I get accepted.

PAT: What do you mean "*if*"? You'll get in, Suz.

SUSAN: I'm not taking any chances. And don't *you* say a word!

PAT: No way! When are you turning it in?

SUSAN: The deadline's tomorrow.

PAT: Tomorrow? Why didn't you wait till the last minute or something?

SUSAN: I was deciding whether or not to do it.

PAT: They asked me to run for class president today.

SUSAN: Are you gonna do it?

PAT: Nah.

SUSAN: Why not?

PAT: 'Cause I'll only lose.

SUSAN: That's Daddy talking.

PAT: Well, this time he's probably right.

SUSAN: No, he's not right. He just has you thinking he is. What you should do is— *[She stops.]*

PAT: What?

SUSAN: Nothing. Forget it.

PAT: No, tell me. What?

SUSAN: I was going to say, what you should do is forget whatever *he* says and do what you want to do. But that's why I waited so long, too. I knew he'd say I wouldn't get in, and I started to believe it.

PAT: Why does he say those things?

SUSAN: Who knows? Maybe because *he* never finished high school. . . . Or because he hates his job. Most parents want their children to do better than they did. But I don't think he feels that way. The important thing is that we don't *believe* the things he says.

PAT: Maybe when I'm your age I'll be able to do that. When I'm with you, it's not so bad. But when I'm alone with him and he starts in—

[The door opens, surprising both of them. Susan

doesn't have time to hide the papers. Their father enters the room.]

FATHER: What are you two doing?

SUSAN: Nothing, Daddy. Just talking.

FATHER: Don't you have anything better to do than waste your time yakking?

PAT: We were talking about school.

[Susan shoots her a look, but Pat quickly shakes her head—she's not going to tell.]

FATHER: Maybe if you didn't spend so much time *talking* about it, you'd do better *at* it.

PAT: They asked me to run for class president.

FATHER: Why bother? You'll never win.

SUSAN: Maybe she will. But if she doesn't run, she'll never know.

FATHER: How would *you* know? Did you ever do it?

SUSAN: No.

FATHER: That's right. All you do is tell other people what they should do. Maybe if you spent more time studying, instead of . . . whatever you waste your time with, you'd be in a position to give advice.

PAT: She got almost straight A's last term.

FATHER: But she didn't get straight A's.

PAT: Four A's and one B. That's—

FATHER: That's not straight A's. When she gets straight A's, you can brag. But she never will. And you want to know why? I'll show you. Here, look at this. *[He goes to the desk and reaches for the papers on it.]* Instead of studying, she wastes her time with . . . *[He discovers the papers Susan tried to hide.]* What's this?

SUSAN: It's nothing. Just some papers.

FATHER: Let me see this. *[He reads the papers.]* Application for The Special School of Performing Arts? You're going to try to get into this school?

SUSAN: I was thinking maybe I'd try, yes.

FATHER: Who put this crazy idea into your head?

SUSAN: Mrs. Harper. My dance teacher. She said she'd sponsor me.

FATHER: What does she know?

SUSAN: She knows a lot. My grades are good enough. And she says I've got the talent to get in.

FATHER: Yeah? Well, if you did get in, you wouldn't stay in. Even if you get the grades, what makes you think you're that good a dancer?

PAT: Mrs. Harper says she is.

FATHER: She's sponsoring her. That tells you what *she* knows!

SUSAN: How do you know I'm not good enough to get in? I got accepted to dance camp this summer. *That* says something!

FATHER: You think you can get into this school?

SUSAN: Yes.

FATHER: You think you're smart enough?

SUSAN: Yes.

FATHER: You think you're that good a dancer?

SUSAN: Yes!

FATHER: OK. Fill out these papers. But if you don't get into the school . . . you don't go to the dance camp.

SUSAN: What if I do get in?

FATHER: Then you get in. And you'll go to your camp.

PAT: What kind of a bet is that? She'll go to the camp if she *doesn't* fill out the papers?

FATHER: It's not a bet. It's a test. To see if she really believes in herself that much. *[to Susan]* But if I were you, I'd stick with a sure thing. For once in your life, be smart. *[He goes to the door.]* A special school! *I* never went to a special school! *[He walks out.]*

SUSAN: I can get into this school.

PAT: So you're going to do it?

SUSAN: I don't know! They only take so many students. Lots of kids who *don't* get in are smart, too. And good dancers. But I really want to study dance there.

PAT: Suz . . . maybe you shouldn't do it. I mean, what if you *don't* get in? You'll lose summer camp, too. Didn't you say that the camp was a great chance to get ahead? That there were talent scouts there? You *know* what he'll be like if you don't get into the school. Maybe it'll be better if you don't try.

SUSAN: Maybe you're right. But maybe that's just Daddy talking.

PAT: You're right. It is. Sorry. But you still have to make a decision. What are you going to do?

SUSAN: . . .

IIII THINKING ABOUT THE PLAY

1. What kind of relationship does Susan have with her father? How do you learn about it before you meet him?

2. Why do you think Susan's father acts the way he does?

3. What effect is he having on Susan and Pat? How do you know?

4. Is he right about his daughters? How do you know?

5. Knowing what you do about Susan and her father, why do you think Susan is even considering applying to the special school?

IIIII THINKING ABOUT THE ENDING

Susan wants to apply to the special school, but her father tells her she's not good enough to get in. Then he tells her she can apply, but if she doesn't get in she can't go to summer dance camp either. Think about what you learned about Susan. Will she apply to the school?

Using what you've learned about the characters, write an ending for the play that includes what Susan does next, her reasons for doing what she does, and her feelings about her decision. Also include Pat's reaction to Susan's decision.

S tarting Over

by Cynthia Benjamin

Characters:
Sharon
Mrs. Henderson
D. J.

Scene One: *the kitchen of the Hendersons' apartment. Sharon lives there with her parents and her 1-year-old son. Mrs. Henderson is washing the dishes. Sharon enters the kitchen. It's 8:00 P.M. and she looks tired.*

SHARON: Hi, Mom. Sorry I didn't get home sooner. *[She sits down on a kitchen chair and takes off her shoes.]* There was no way I could leave the store until we finished the inventory.

MRS. HENDERSON: There's nothing to apologize for. I gave Benjamin his dinner. Your father bathed him and put him to sleep. That little boy is sure getting fussy.

SHARON: You're telling me. He had me up all night.

MRS. HENDERSON: *[smiling]* Babies can do that. But I have to tell you, your dad gets a real kick out of him. Says he reminds him of Rick at his age.

SHARON: Well, my brother turned out OK, so I guess Benjamin will, too. *[She gets up and crosses to the kitchen door.]*

MRS. HENDERSON: Now where are you going? I bet you haven't had any dinner.

SHARON: Right. That meeting with my guidance counselor lasted until 4:00. Then I went right to work. But I have to see Benjamin.

MRS. HENDERSON: I'll reheat your dinner. It should be ready soon. *[She takes a plate of food from the refrigerator.]*

SHARON: Thanks, Mom.

[She leaves. Mrs. Henderson puts the plate into the oven. Sharon returns to the kitchen while her mother prepares her dinner.] Mom, let me do that.

MRS. HENDERSON: You sit down. You've done enough today. How's Benjamin?

SHARON: Sleeping. Doesn't seem to have a care in the world.

MRS. HENDERSON: I should hope not. Not at 1 year old. *[She puts a salad on the table.]*

SHARON: Give me a minute. For the first time in my life I'm too tired to eat. *[rubbing her feet]* I haven't had a break all day.

MRS. HENDERSON: Can you get to bed early tonight?

SHARON: No way. I have to study for my English final. If Benjamin lets me, that is. But there is good news. My guidance counselor told me the college scholarship is looking good.

MRS. HENDERSON: Honey, that's wonderful. Wait until I tell your father.

SHARON: Let's not say anything yet. It's been tough for Dad since the plant closed. If the scholarship doesn't happen, I don't want him to be disappointed.

MRS. HENDERSON: Let's think positively about this. It *is* going to come through. Next year you *are* going to City College. After everything you've been through, you deserve it.

SHARON: *[kissing her mother]* Thanks, mom. That means a lot to me. *[Sharon opens the oven door to check on her dinner.]*

MRS. HENDERSON: I thought you weren't hungry.

SHARON: *[laughing]* Just talking about going to college made me feel better.

MRS. HENDERSON: I'm just sorry your father and I can't help you with the expenses.

SHARON: I don't expect you to. You've done enough for Benjamin already. His medical bills have been pretty high. *[hugging her mother]* But one day I'm going to pay you back.

MRS. HENDERSON: We don't want that. You and Benjamin have brought a lot of joy into our lives. Just think. In four more years, you'll have your college degree.

SHARON: Well, it might take longer than that.

MRS. HENDERSON: Why? You've made up the credits you lost when you left school.

SHARON: That's not the problem. The scholarship won't cover everything. So I'll have to go to college part-time and keep working at the store.

MRS. HENDERSON: *[looking angry]* It's not fair. When I think of that D. J., I could—

SHARON: Mom, please. We've been through this before. I'm responsible for myself and Benjamin. D. J. isn't a part of my life anymore.
[Mrs. Henderson takes the plate out of the oven and puts it on the table.]

MRS. HENDERSON: I wasn't sure if I should say anything to you, but—

SHARON: I know what you're going to say, Mom. It wasn't a

ghost. D. J.'s back, all right. He was waiting for me after school yesterday.

MRS. HENDERSON: Oh, Sharon. You didn't talk to him.

SHARON: I have nothing to say. Not after he turned his back on me and his child.

MRS. HENDERSON: Well, I'd like to say a few words to him myself. And if I do, D. J. better watch out.

SHARON: Mom, don't. Please. It's not going to change anything to stay angry at him. He was young.

MRS. HENDERSON: He was 17, two years older than you were. That's old enough to know right from wrong. Running out on your girlfriend when she's pregnant is wrong.

SHARON: I don't want to talk about it now. I'm just too tired to think straight.

[Mrs. Henderson watches Sharon eating. She brushes away a lock of hair that's fallen in her face.]

MRS. HENDERSON: Give yourself a break tonight. You can study for that exam tomorrow.

SHARON: I can't. I have to work late again at the store.

[The doorbell rings. Sharon starts to get up from the kitchen table.]

MRS. HENDERSON: Finish your dinner. I'll get it.

[Mrs. Henderson leaves the kitchen. Sharon finishes her dinner and clears the table.]

SHARON: Mom, who is it?

[D. J. follows Mrs. Henderson into the kitchen. He's tall and good-looking, wearing jeans and a work shirt.]

MRS. HENDERSON: *[in an icy voice]* We have a visitor, Sharon. I tried persuading him to leave.

D. J.: Mrs. Henderson, I have to talk to her. *[He faces*

Sharon. They don't speak for several seconds.] I'd like to see Benjamin.

MRS. HENDERSON: *[to D. J.]* Now? You should have seen him come into this world.

SHARON: Mother, stop it.

D. J.: No, she's right. *[to Mrs. Henderson]* After the way I acted, I have no right to ask Sharon for anything. But Benjamin's my son, too. I have to see him. *[to Sharon]* Please . . . just for a little while.

SHARON: *[to D. J.]* All right. He's sleeping now. But I'll take you to his room. Just be sure not to wake him.

MRS. HENDERSON: *[sadly]* Sharon, don't let yourself believe him. Not again. *[She starts washing the dishes in the sink.]*

SHARON: I'll do that.

MRS. HENDERSON: You were up at 6:00 to take care of Benjamin and study. Then you went to school and worked until 8:00. *[She turns and glares at D. J.]* You've done more than your share today.

[She turns her back on D. J. and Sharon. Sharon and D. J. leave the kitchen. A few seconds later, Sharon returns alone.]

SHARON: I couldn't refuse to let him look at his own son.

MRS. HENDERSON: You have no sense where D. J.'s concerned. You never did. *[She folds the dish towel.]* Well, at least he's out of our lives.

SHARON: Not just yet. He's still in Benjamin's room. I told him he could stay so we could talk things over.

MRS. HENDERSON: *[disappointed]* Oh, Sharon. Why?

SHARON: Because it's important to me and to D. J. I want to hear what he has to say.

[D. J. enters the kitchen.]

MRS. HENDERSON: *[to Sharon]* I'll be in the living room.
[She walks past D. J. without looking at him.]

SHARON: I'm sorry about that.

D. J.: That's all right. I can understand how she feels. After what I did to you and Benjamin, she should be angry.

SHARON: *[quietly]* Why did you come back?

D. J.: To say I'm sorry. I can't even explain why I ran out on you. I don't understand it myself.

SHARON: Do you understand how I felt? Fifteen years old and pregnant. If it hadn't been for my parents, I don't know what I would have done.

D. J.: I know this doesn't help, but I did come back once before. It was two months before Benjamin was born.

SHARON: Why didn't you come to see me?

D. J.: I was too ashamed and scared. I just couldn't handle it.

SHARON: Well, I didn't have that choice. I was the one who

was pregnant. I had Benjamin. After he was born, you know what happened. I dropped out of school. Those first few months were really tough for me, for all of us.

D. J.: I know.

SHARON: How can you? Taking care of an infant isn't like playing with some cute little doll. It's hard work.

D. J.: That's why I came back. There's no way you should be working like this. You go to school, work, and take care of a baby. It's too much.

SHARON: Maybe you have a better idea?

D. J.: I want to take care of him and you. No matter what's happened, he's my son, too. And I have rights where he's concerned.

SHARON: Those rights come with responsibilities.

D. J.: I know that. That's what I'm trying to tell you Nothing's changed since the last time we were together. I still love you.

SHARON: I don't believe it.

D.J.: Let me prove it to you. Marry me.

[Sharon is about to cry. She just shakes her head.]

D.J.: It's about time we were a family. I have my high school diploma and a good job at the factory. In another year, I might be a foreman.

SHARON: D. J., my mother was right. You always were a big talker.

[D. J. takes out his wallet and shows her his I.D. card.]

D. J.: *[smiling]* OK, maybe it will take two years to be a foreman. But the job is solid. Look, here's my I.D. card. There's some money in the bank. I've been saving every penny.

SHARON: Why?

D. J.: For you and Benjamin. For our future together.
[He touches her cheek. She starts to pull back. Then she stops.] I might be a big talker sometimes. I don't know why I do it. Guess I like feeling important. But what I said before . . . about loving you. That wasn't talk.

SHARON: I know. *[They kiss.]*

D. J.: Marry me, Sharon.

SHARON: *[suddenly]* What about my family? They've been so good to me. No matter what, they helped me. Besides, this is Benjamin's home, too. The only home he knows.

D. J.: He'll have a new home, with his father and his mother.

SHARON: For how long? How do I know you won't run out on us?

D. J.: Because things are different now. I swear it.

SHARON: It's all too much too fast. I've worked hard to get my life back together. I made so many plans. Next year I'm starting college, you know.

D. J.: How can you go to school and take care of Benjamin?

SHARON: It's just part-time at first.

D. J.: Don't you see? You won't have to worry about college and work now. I'll take care of the two of you. It's what I should have been doing all along. Just give me a chance.

SHARON: I have to think. Right now, everything's mixed up.

D. J.: No. The more you think, the less chance we have of getting back together. I want your answer now.
[Sharon looks at D. J.]

IIII■THINKING ABOUT THE PLAY

1. Do you think that D. J. has changed? Explain your answer.

2. How would you compare Sharon's character with D. J.'s?

3. How does Sharon feel about D. J. now compared to how she felt about him in the past?

4. How has Sharon changed since she had the baby?

5. Why does Mrs. Henderson say, "Sharon, don't let yourself believe him. Not again."?

IIII■THINKING ABOUT THE ENDING

Sharon has many different feelings about D. J. Then he suddenly appears and asks her to marry him. Think about what you have learned about Sharon and about D. J. Then consider Sharon's goals. Do you think she and D. J. have similar ambitions? What might her life be like if she says no? Is there another possibility?

After thinking about Sharon and D. J.'s past relationship, decide what she will do. Then write an ending to the play that shows how this decision will affect both of them.

Marcella

by Chiori Santiago

Characters:
Marcella
Mother
Darcy

Scene: *the living room and kitchen of Marcella's home. Marcella lives with her mother and her 4-year-old sister, Darcy. Marcella's mother is a single parent who works two part-time jobs. While she's at work, Marcella is in charge of the home and takes care of Darcy. In the living room is a fold-out sofa where Marcella and Darcy sleep.*

MOTHER: *[offstage]* Marcella! Marcella, get up and make that bed now!

[Marcella is under a heap of blankets. She begins to stir.]

DARCY: Ow, you kicked me.

MARCELLA: It's time to get up, anyway, lazy bum.

DARCY: *[sitting up]* Mom! Marcella's calling me names!

MOTHER: *[coming into the room. She has taken a shower and is wearing a robe and toweling her hair dry.]* Can't I get through one morning without having to deal with you two? Work it out! Pretend I'm not here!

MARCELLA: *[mumbling]* You never are here.

MOTHER: What? If you want me to hear you, speak up. If not,

shut up. I'm not putting up with this whining any more. Get up and fix that bed.

MARCELLA: Mom, it's Saturday.

MOTHER: So? You have a lot to do today. I want this house clean when I get home, and that includes dishes, sweeping up, and the laundry. Do you hear me, Marcella?

MARCELLA: OK, OK.

[Her mother disappears into the bathroom. Marcella goes to the kitchen to make a pot of coffee.]

MOTHER: *[offstage]* You making coffee?

MARCELLA: *[yawning]* Yeah. You want some?

MOTHER: *[offstage]* I sure do, honey. Thanks.

[Darcy has turned on the TV. She sits on the fold-out sofa, wrapped in a blanket and sucking her thumb, watching cartoons. Marcella stands in the kitchen in her nightgown, waiting for the coffee machine to finish brewing.]

MARCELLA: *[to the audience]* Welcome to my house. Loud, isn't it? There are just the three of us, Mom, Darcy, and me. But sometimes I think we make enough noise for a whole big family. Everyone talks at the top of their lungs. Maybe it's because something is always going on. The TV's on or the radio. Or the rush-hour traffic is going by outside. Sometimes it's because Mom never comes into the room to talk to us; she shouts from whatever part of the aparment she's in. "Marcella, come here!" "Marcella, get off the phone!" I hardly ever see her smile, never mind talk in a soft voice. I remember her singing me lullabies when I was Darcy's age. But that was a long time ago. Since Darcy was born, Mom is crabbier than ever. She punishes me for every little thing. But she doesn't scare me like she used to.

MOTHER: *[walking into the kitchen, dressed for work]* Oh,

great, coffee. *[Marcella pours her a cup without speaking.]* You didn't use too much coffee, did you? It's getting expensive, you know. *[Marcella rolls her eyes and shrugs.]* Don't make faces at me, Marcella.

MARCELLA: *[throwing up her hands]* You never trust anything I do! You always treat me like I'm such a jerk, even when I'm helping you!

MOTHER: *[setting down her coffee cup]* Are you shouting at me? Since when do you pay the bills around here? Are you the one working two jobs to put a roof over our heads?

MARCELLA: OK, Mom, please, it's too early in the morning.

MOTHER: Oh, poor Marcella has to help her mother once a week. Once a week, that's all. All you have to do around here is a little housecleaning, a little baby-sitting, stuff anyone could do. Do you cook? No. Do you iron clothes? No. I get up early every single morning to earn a living. Why? Because I have two lazy kids. "Mom, I need new shoes." "Mom, I need money for a field trip." Mom this and Mom that. When do I get to live my life? *[Marcella sits at the dining table while her mother is talking. She hunches over her coffee cup, trying to ignore her mother.]* You see? You don't even have the decency and respect to listen to me. *[Mother storms out of the kitchen.]*

MARCELLA: *[to the audience]* Do you see what I mean? She hates me. My own mother. Sometimes she acts like she wishes I had never been born. She likes Darcy better. She liked Darcy's dad better than my dad. I haven't seen my dad since I was in kindergarten. She says I look just like him. She says he was a bum. She thinks I'm just like him. Darcy's lucky. Her dad still calls her up and sends her toys for Christmas. She doesn't know how lucky she is. When I was little, Mom spanked me with a hairbrush and I'd hardly cry. But then, she would do the worst thing. The thing that scared me most. She would grab me by the wrist. She would pull me along, talking the whole time. "Don't you know things cost money? I'll teach you to be responsible," she'd say. And she would open the door to the broom closet in the kitchen. She'd make me sit in there. She'd close the door. Then she'd set the timer in the kitchen. "Ten minutes," she'd say. "Think about why you're in there." I'm never going to be like Mom when I have kids. *[Marcella goes out to the living room and sits down next to Darcy.]* Hi, Darcy. What're you watching? *[Darcy squeals and turns her head away.]* Come on, Darcy, get your finger out of your mouth. *[Marcella leans over and tries to pull her sister's thumb from her mouth.]*

DARCY: *[shouting]* Leave me alone! I'm watching cartoons, all right?

MOTHER: *[entering the room]* Are you bothering your sister now? Darcy, turn that TV off. *[Darcy ignores her. Mother rummages around the bookshelf and then the coffee table.]* Have you seen my keys?

MARCELLA: They were on the table last night.

MOTHER: Can't I put something down once and have it be there when I get back?

MARCELLA: Maybe if we put a nail on the back of the door we could hang our keys there and—

MOTHER: Can't you just shut up and give me a hand?

MARCELLA: *[standing]* Can't you just get organized? No wonder Darcy's dad couldn't stand it around here. You're always yelling and nagging and blaming everyone, and you act like you're so perfect—

[Darcy puts her hands over her ears as their mother starts yelling, too. Suddenly, Mother takes off one of her shoes and tries to hit Marcella. Marcella dives under a pillow to take cover, and her mother beats the pillow. Darcy crawls under the coffee table. After a few half-hearted blows, Marcella's mother stops.]

She straightens and wipes away tears. Then she sighs. There is a long moment of silence.]

DARCY: Mom, I found your keys. *[She crawls from under the table.]*

MOTHER: *[trying to compose herself]* Thanks, baby. Marcella? *[She reaches out to touch Marcella's foot. Marcella, still hiding under the pillow, pulls away.]* Listen, I'm sorry. I don't know—sometimes you just drive me crazy. *[She puts on her shoe.]* I don't know. Maybe I'm just working too hard—it's just—I really need your help, Marcella. I'm sorry I lost my temper. *[She looks at Marcella, who is still hiding under the pillow.]* Well. OK. Darcy, come say good-bye. *[She gets up and goes to the door.]* I'll see you guys later. Be good. Darcy, help your sister, you hear? *[Mother leaves.]*

MARCELLA: *[to the audience, her head still under the pillow]* It was dark in there. Darker than this. I was lonely, so lonely. I was afraid of spiders. I thought if I sat real still, they wouldn't see me or bite me. When I was little, I used to cry in the broom closet. I used to scream for Mom to let me out. She never did, not until I heard the timer ring. I tried to get out, but she'd put a chair across the door or something. When she let me out, she'd say, "I hope that gave you something to think about." When I got older, I swallowed my tears. I kept my eyes shut in the broom closet. I hated it. But it made me tough. Sometimes I don't feel a thing.

DARCY: Marcella, are you OK?

MARCELLA: *[sitting up, clutching the pillow.]* Yeah. She didn't even touch me. *[She hits Darcy with the pillow.]*

DARCY: *[laughing]* Hey! *[She grabs the other pillow and hits Marcella.]*

MARCELLA: Got you back! *[They have a pillow fight. At one point, Darcy smacks Marcella in the head when she isn't expecting it.]* Darcy! That hurt. *[She hits Darcy with the pillow again and again. Darcy starts crying.]* Crybaby. Cut it out, Darcy, I didn't hurt you. Come on. We'd better start cleaning up. Give me a hand. *[She begins folding blankets.]*

DARCY: No. I hate you. You're mean.

MARCELLA: I hate you, too. Get off the bed. *[She pushes Darcy off the bed and folds it into the sofa. She begins to straighten the room.]* Go get the broom, will you, so I can sweep up in here.

DARCY: No.

MARCELLA: Darcy, get the broom. *[Darcy doesn't move.]* Darcy, do what I tell you! *[Darcy still doesn't move.]* You brat! *[Marcella grabs her sister and shakes her.]*

DARCY: Leave me alone! You're hurting me! I'm telling!

MARCELLA: You don't want to help me? Fine. I'll show you what I can do with a broom. You're going to have a lot more to cry about. I'm giving you one more chance. Darcy, go get the broom!

DARCY: Leave me alone!

MARCELLA: That's it. I've had it. Now you're going to get punished. Just because you made me get that broom when I have better things to do. And you're going to help me clean up. I'll make you.

[Marcella marches to the broom closet.]

I'm going to give you something to think about!

[Marcella opens the door of the closet. She hesitates and then . . .]

▌▌▌▌ THINKING ABOUT THE PLAY

1. Why do you think Marcella's mother acts the way she does?
2. How do you think Marcella feels about Darcy?
3. Does Marcella's mother feel bad after she hits Marcella with her shoe? How do you know this?
4. Why does Marcella threaten Darcy?
5. Is there anything Marcella can do to improve the relationships in her family?

Marcella is caught in a pattern of violence. When her mother punishes her, Marcella thinks it is all right to punish her sister. At the same time, she remembers how lonely, scared, and hurt she felt as a little girl when she was locked in the broom closet.

Using what you know about Marcella, write an ending to the play in which she rethinks the need to punish Darcy or decides that harsh punishment is the proper way to discipline a child.